Squiggle Art Drawing Book

By J. E. Martin

Directions

On each page, use pencils, pens, markers, crayons, or another form of art to turn the squiggle into your own unique drawing, design, story, or visual scene!

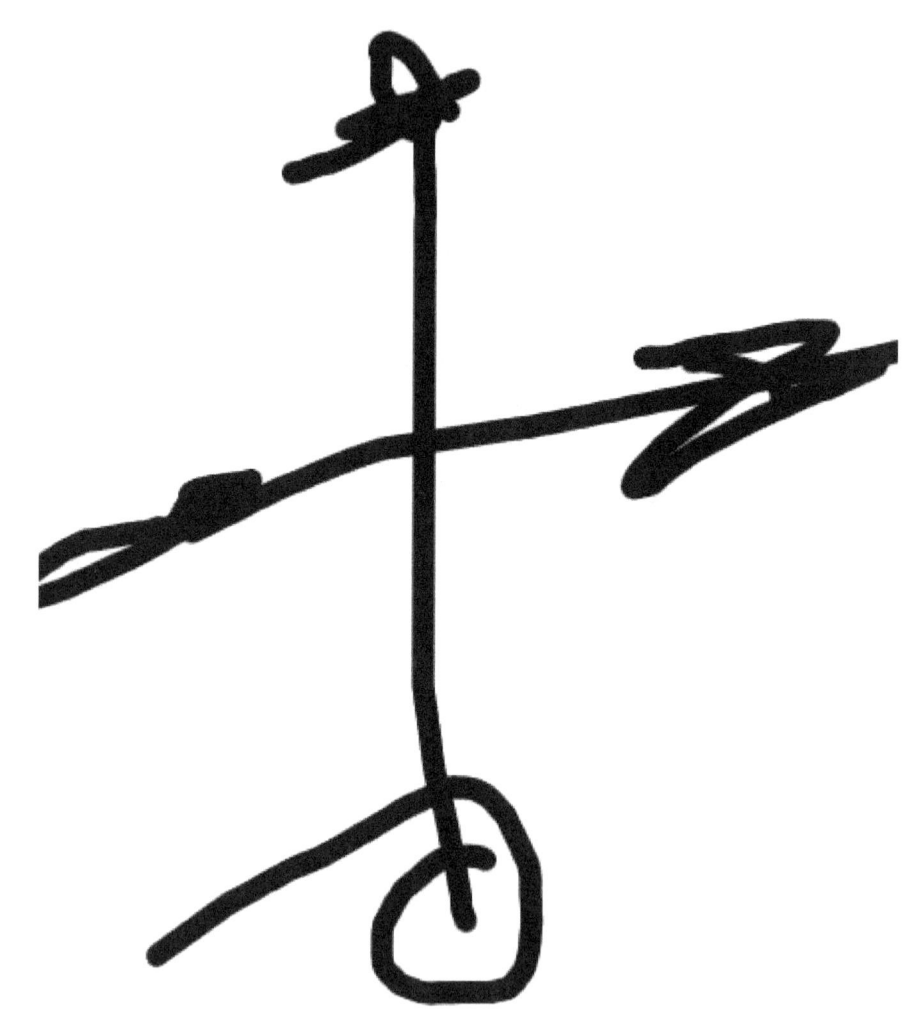

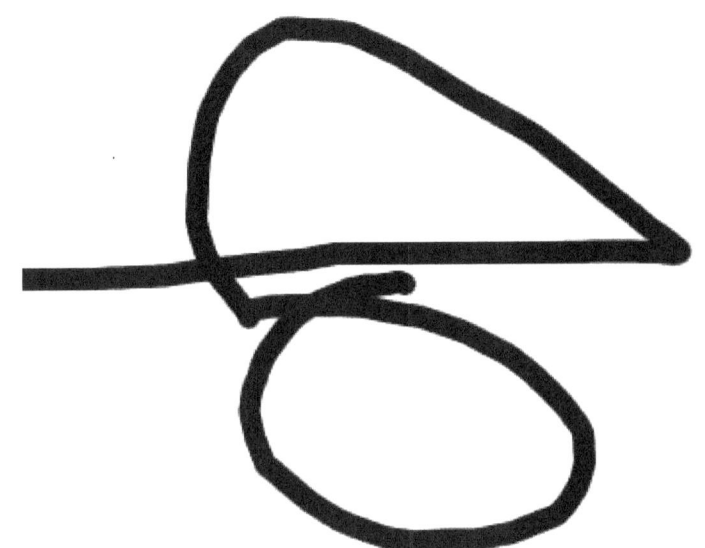

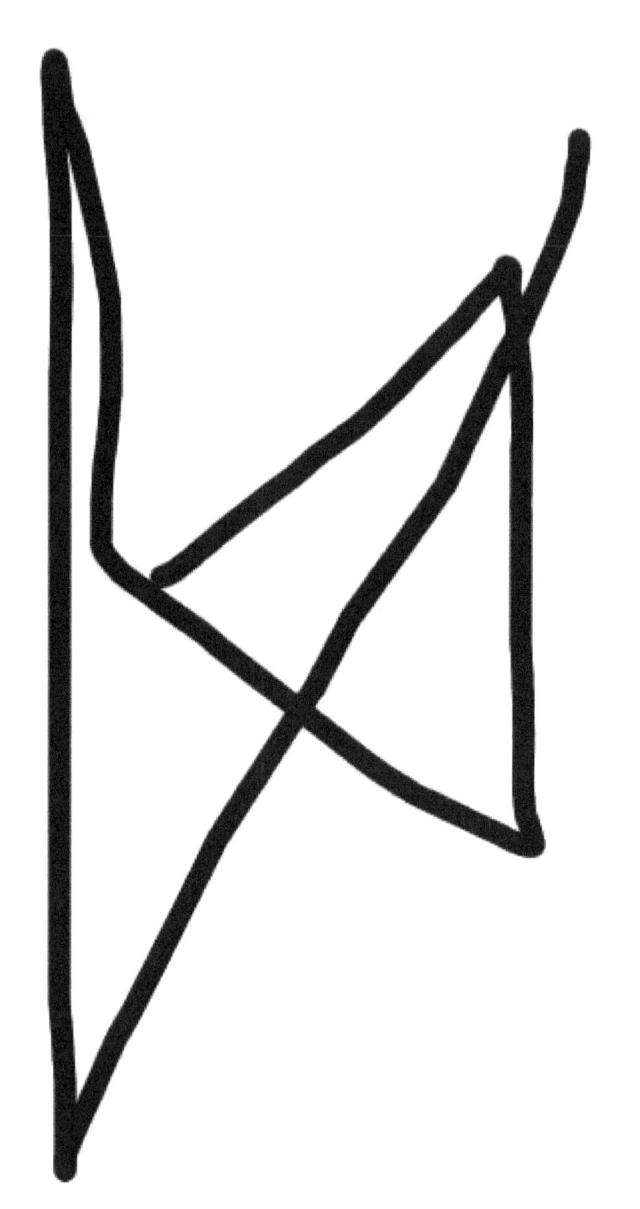

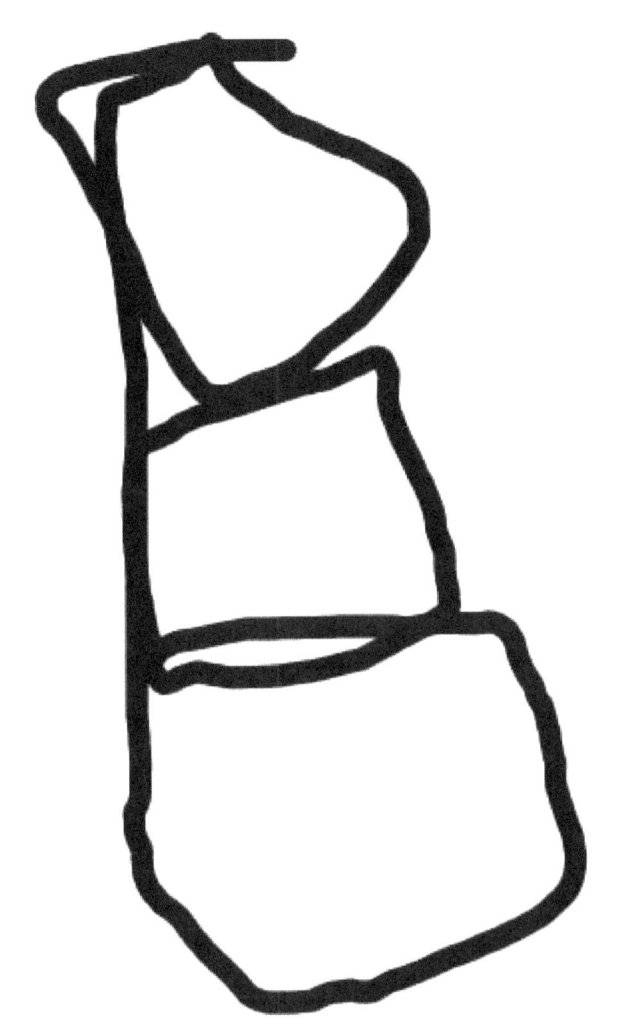

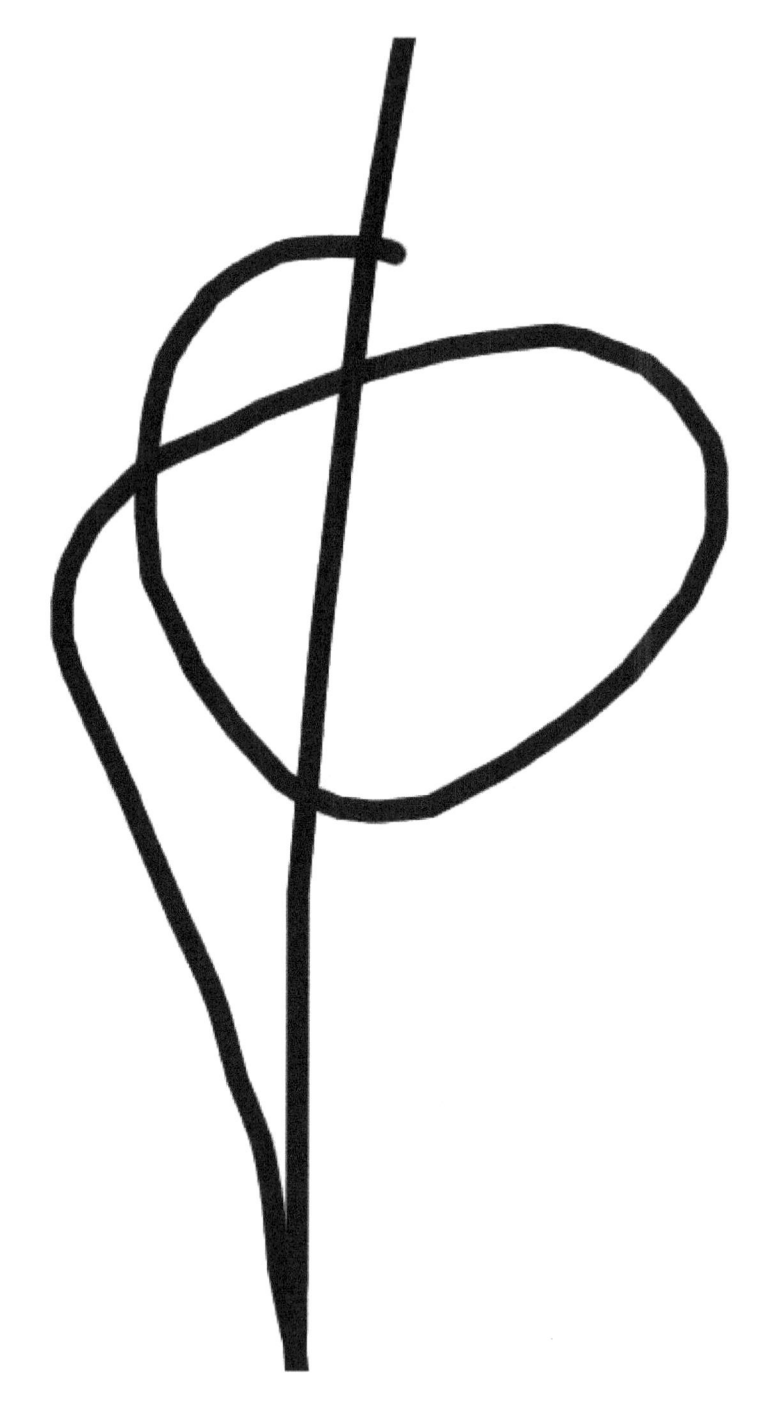

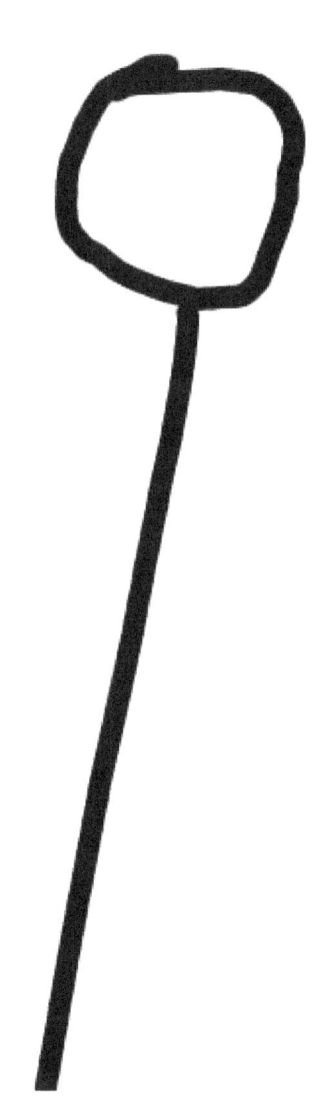

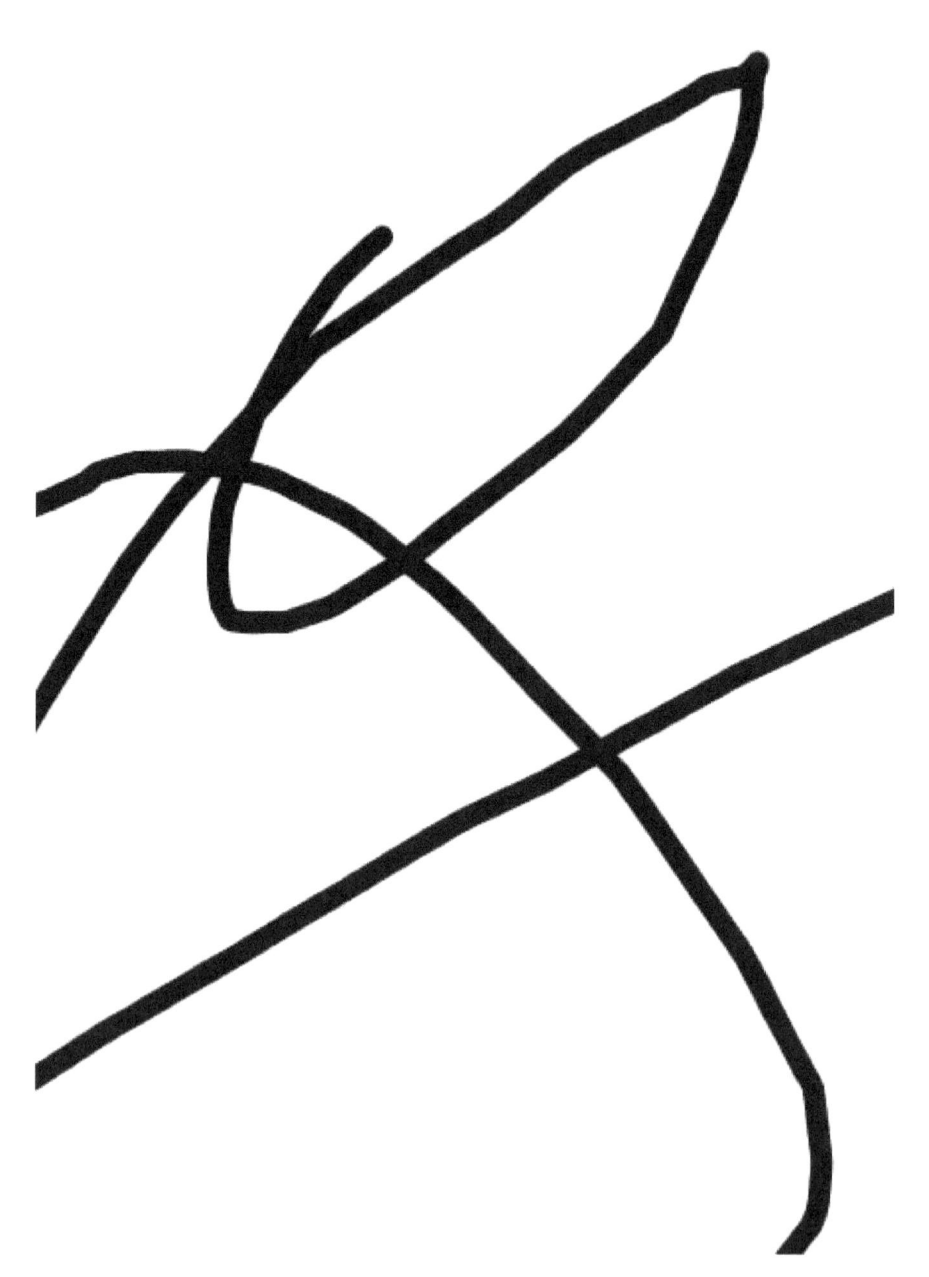

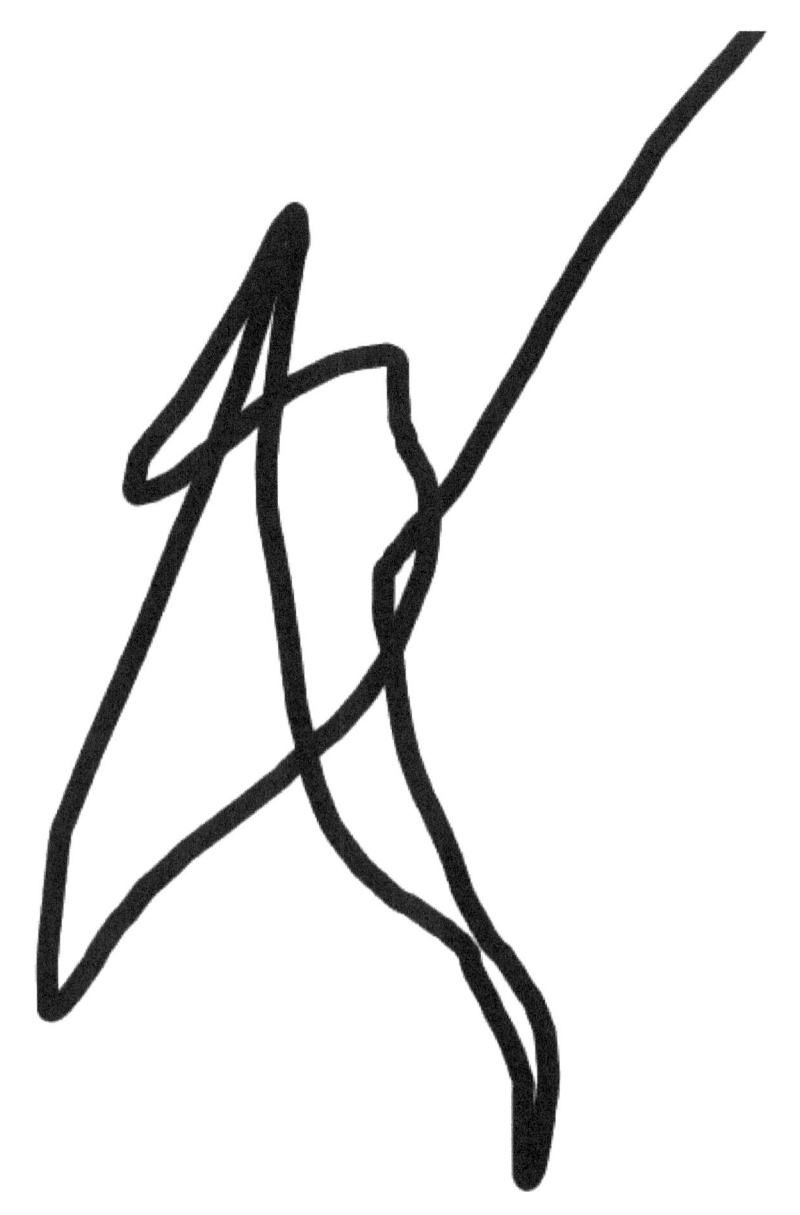

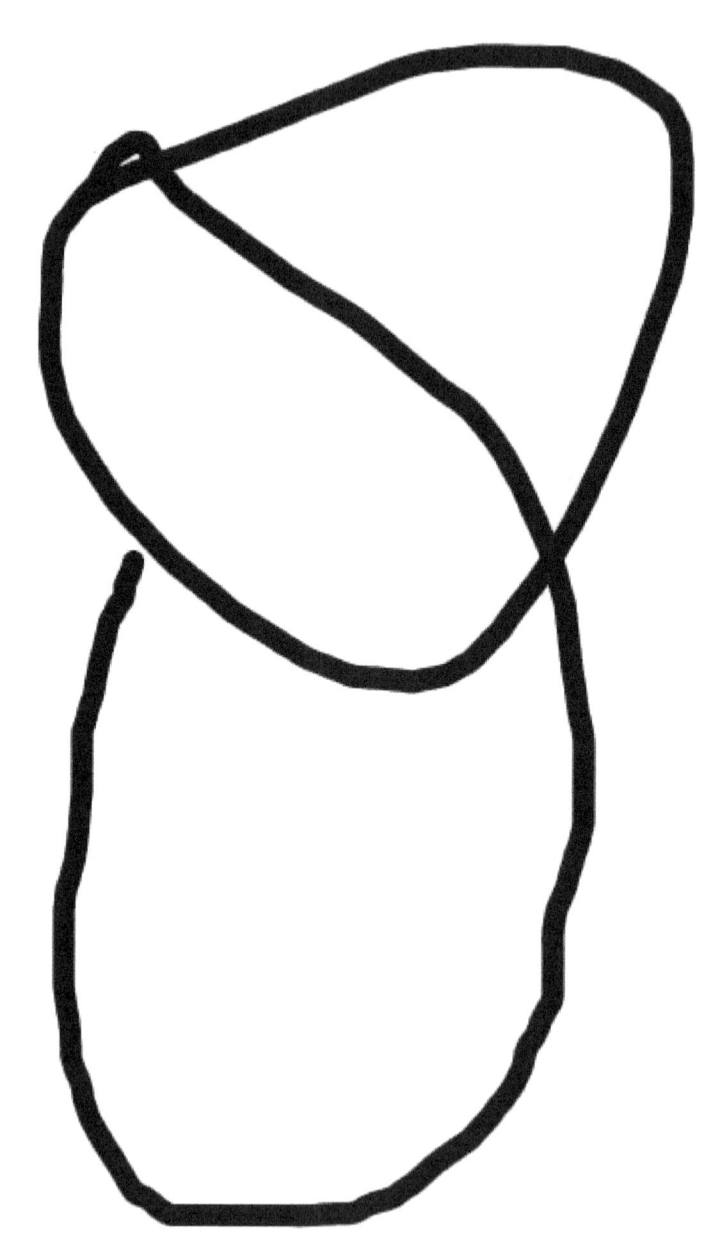

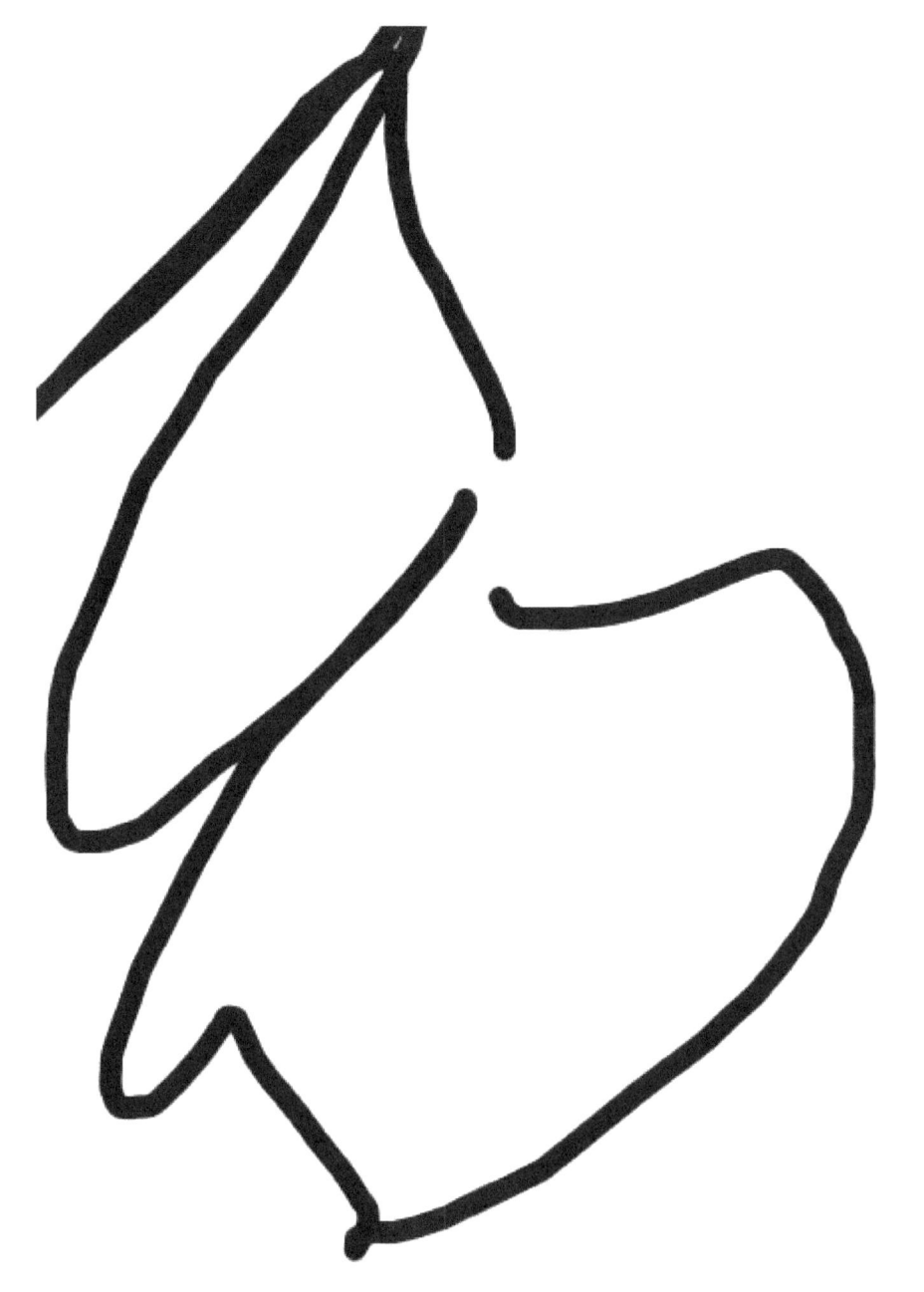

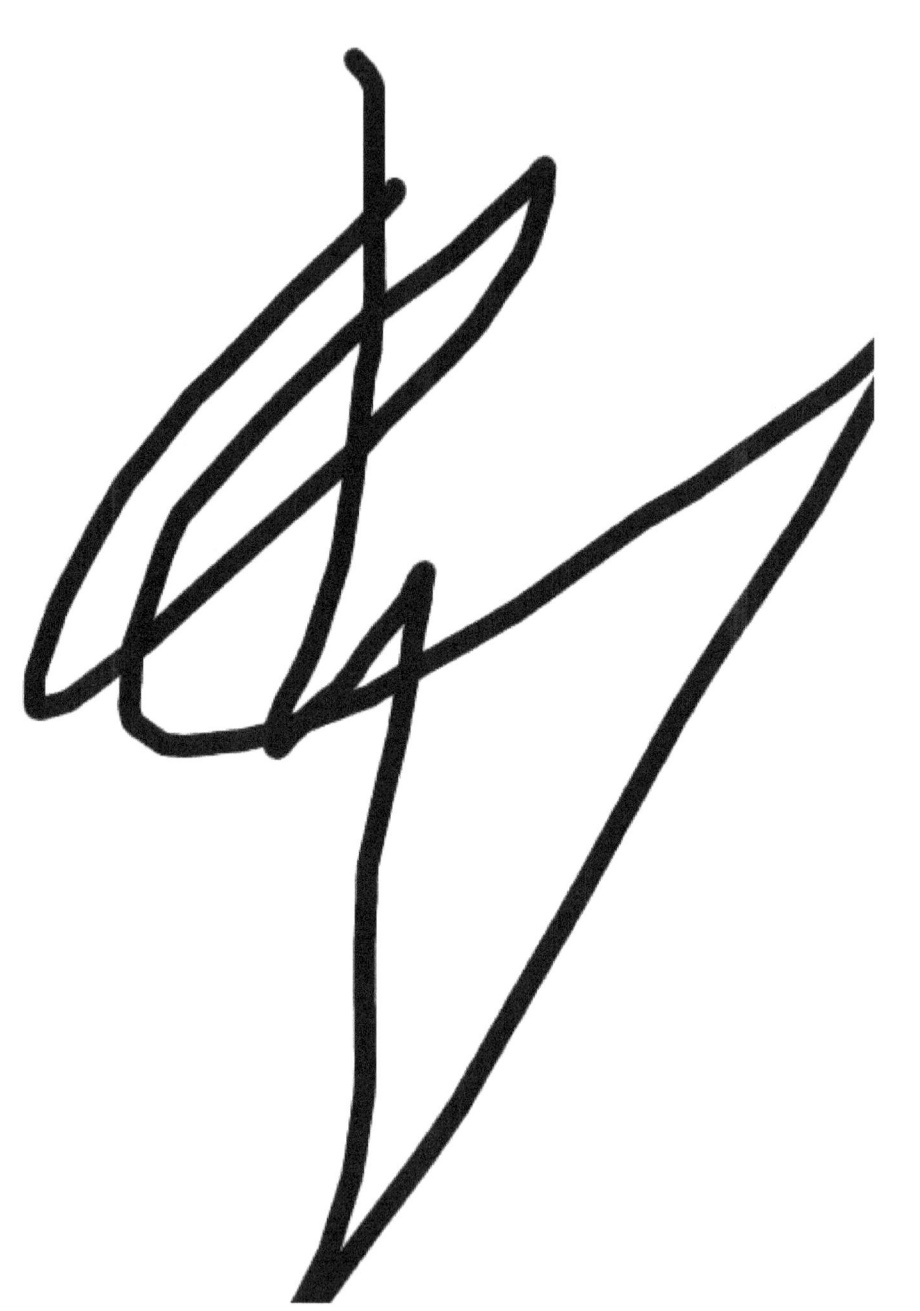

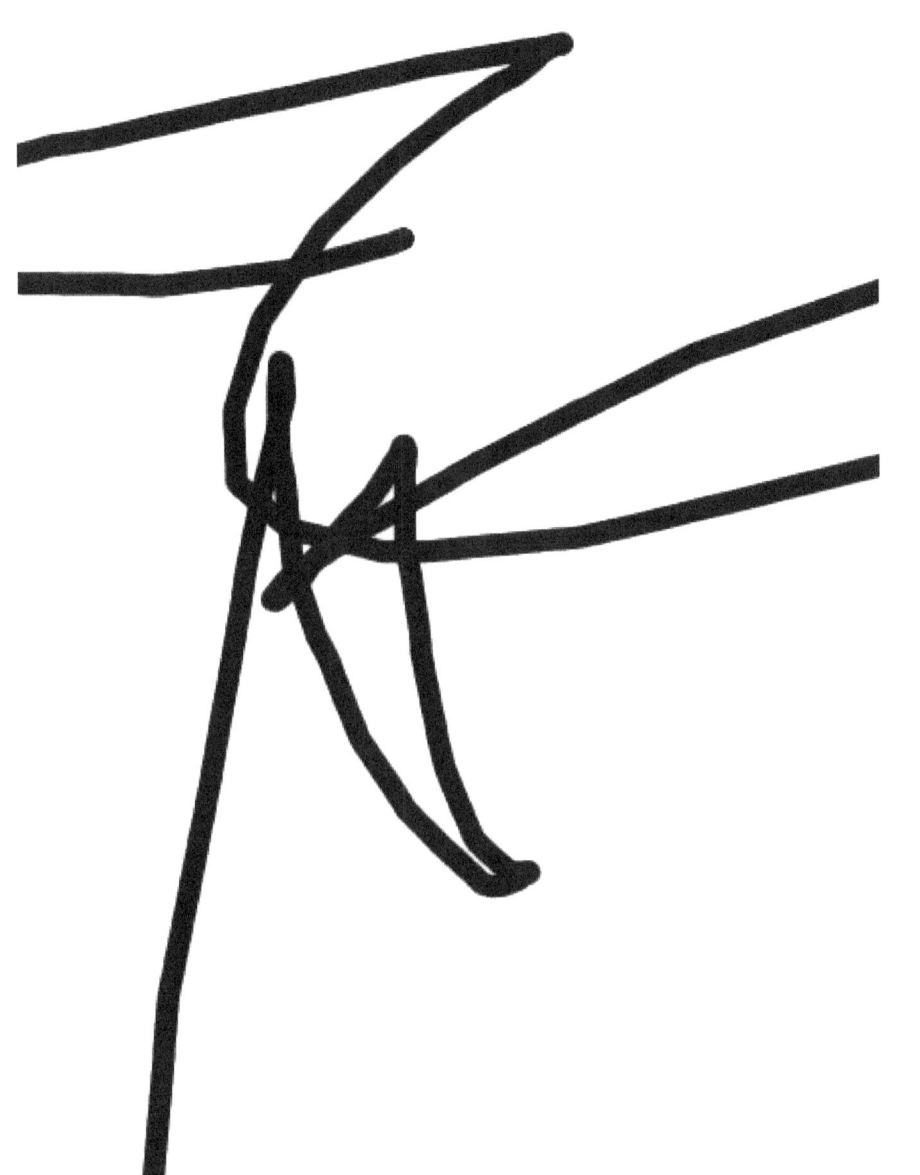

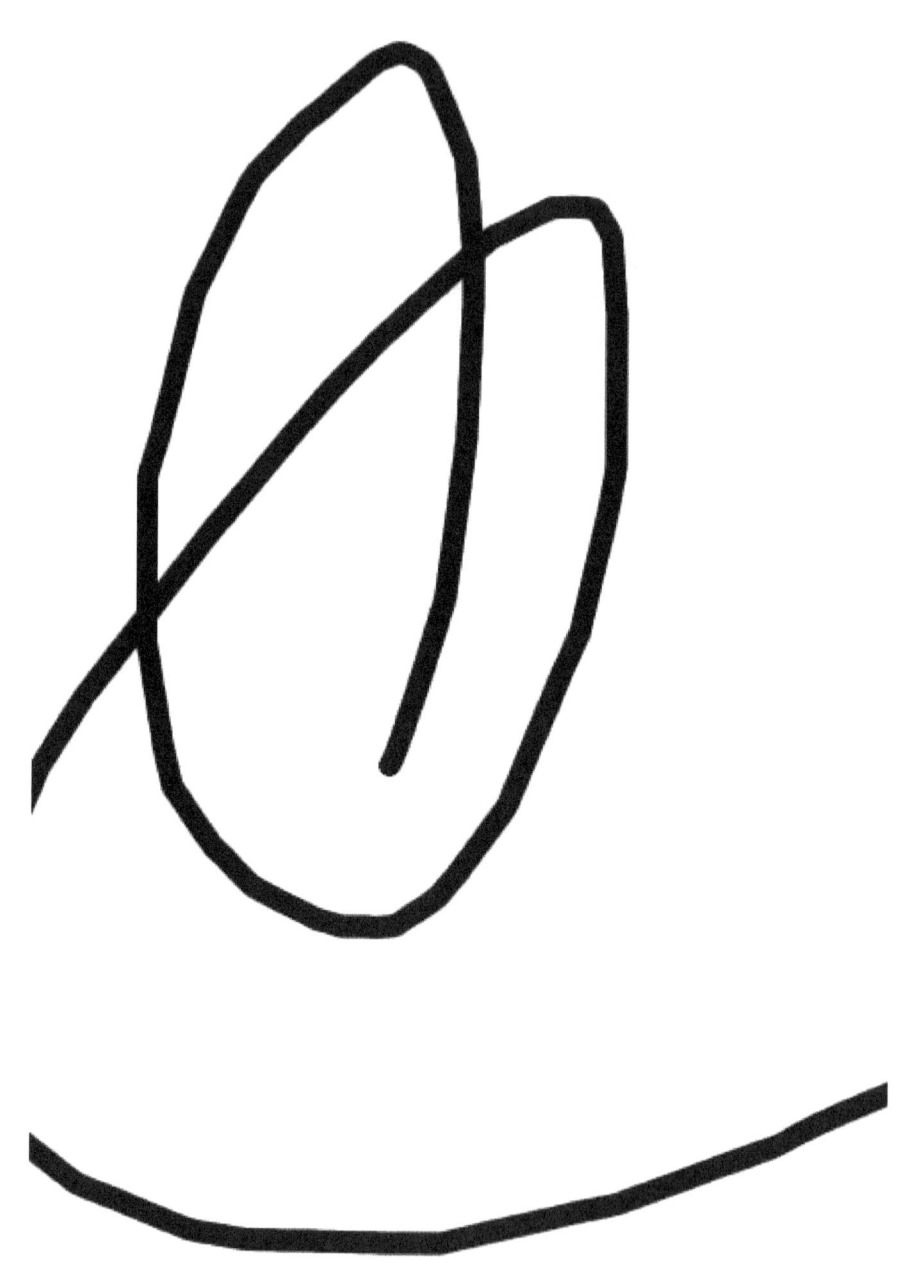

七 初

四 月

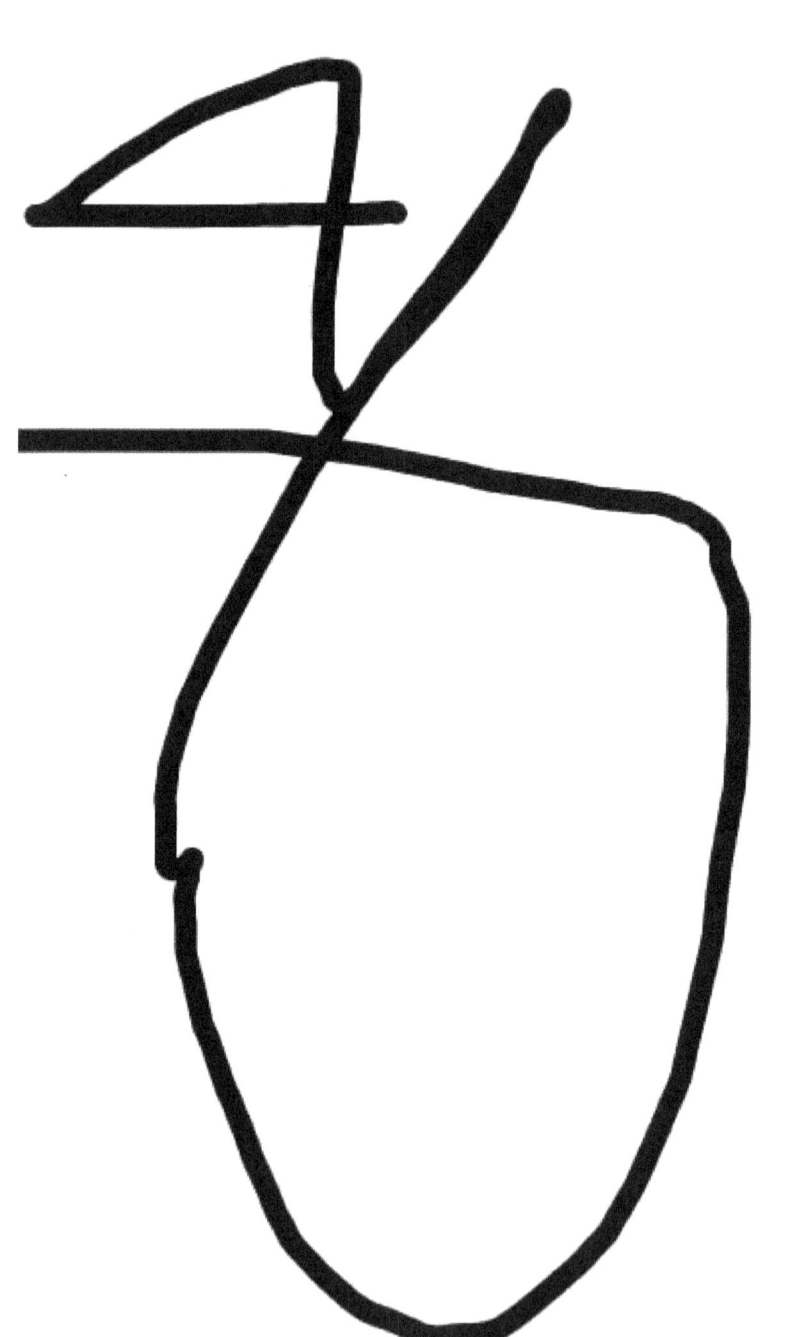

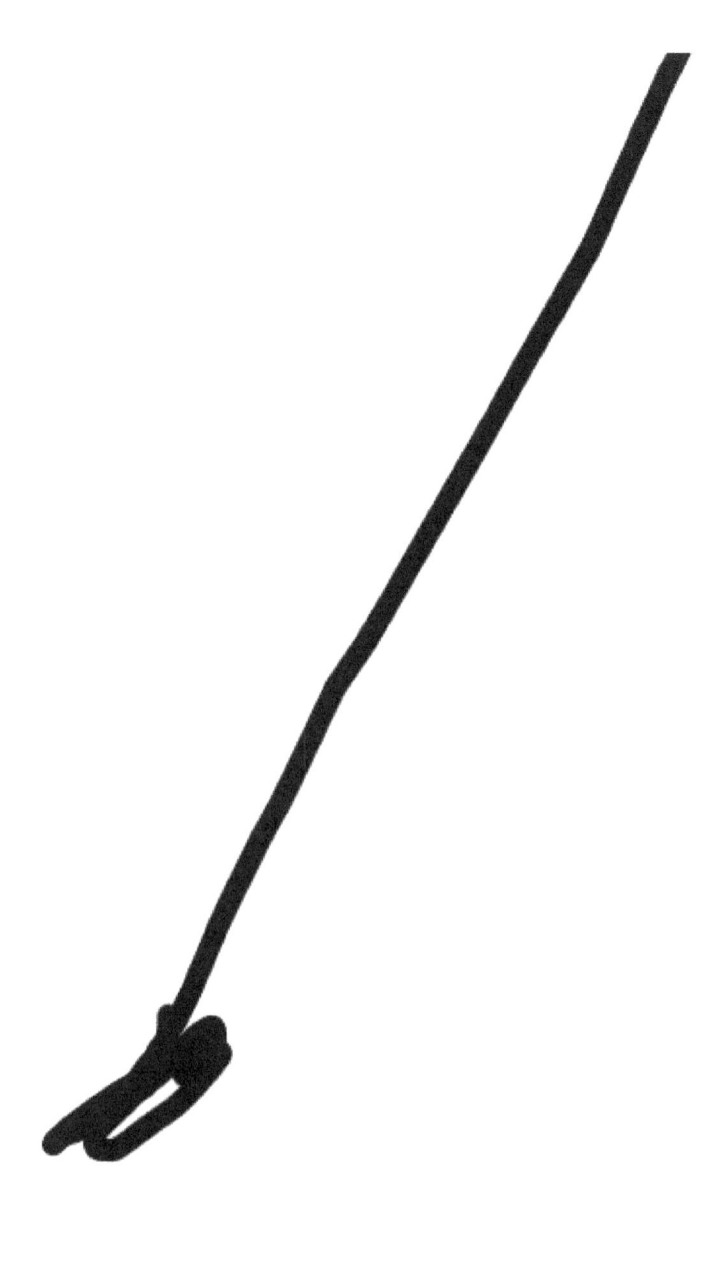

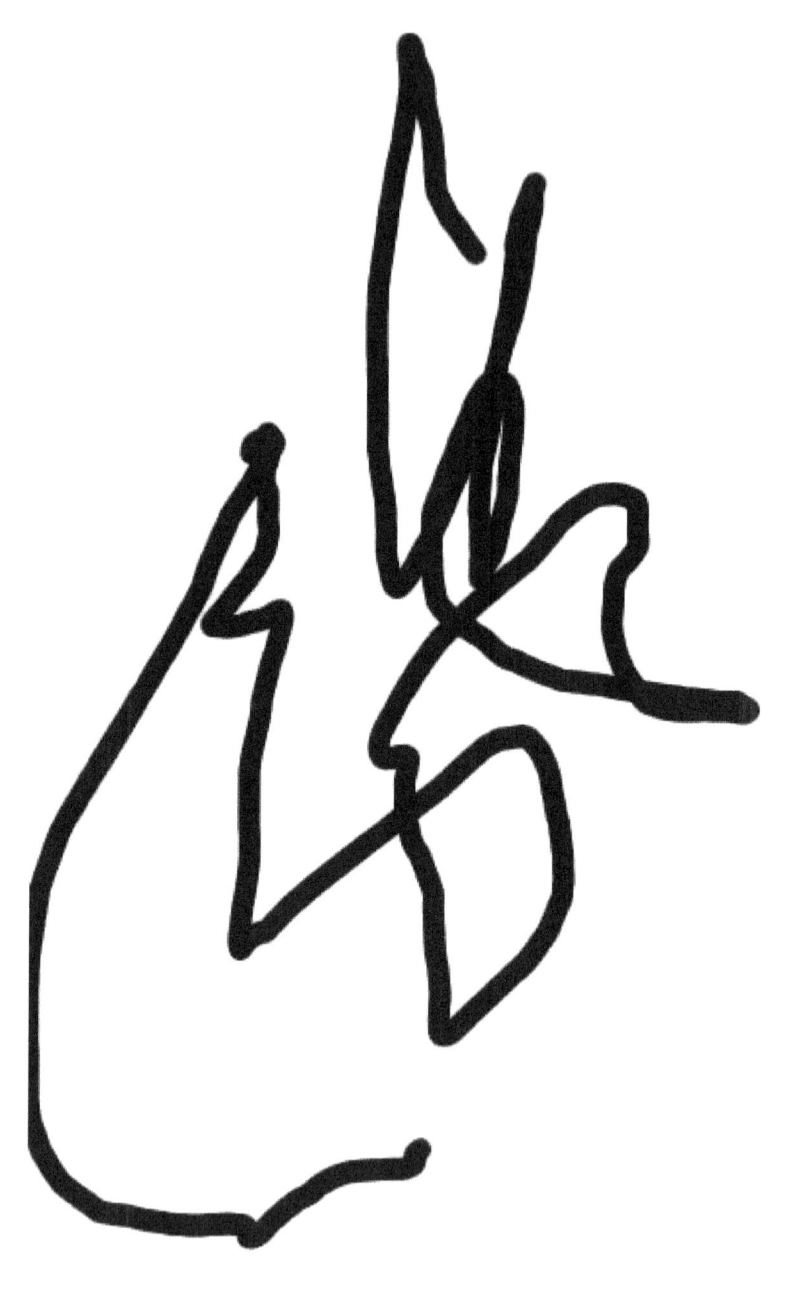

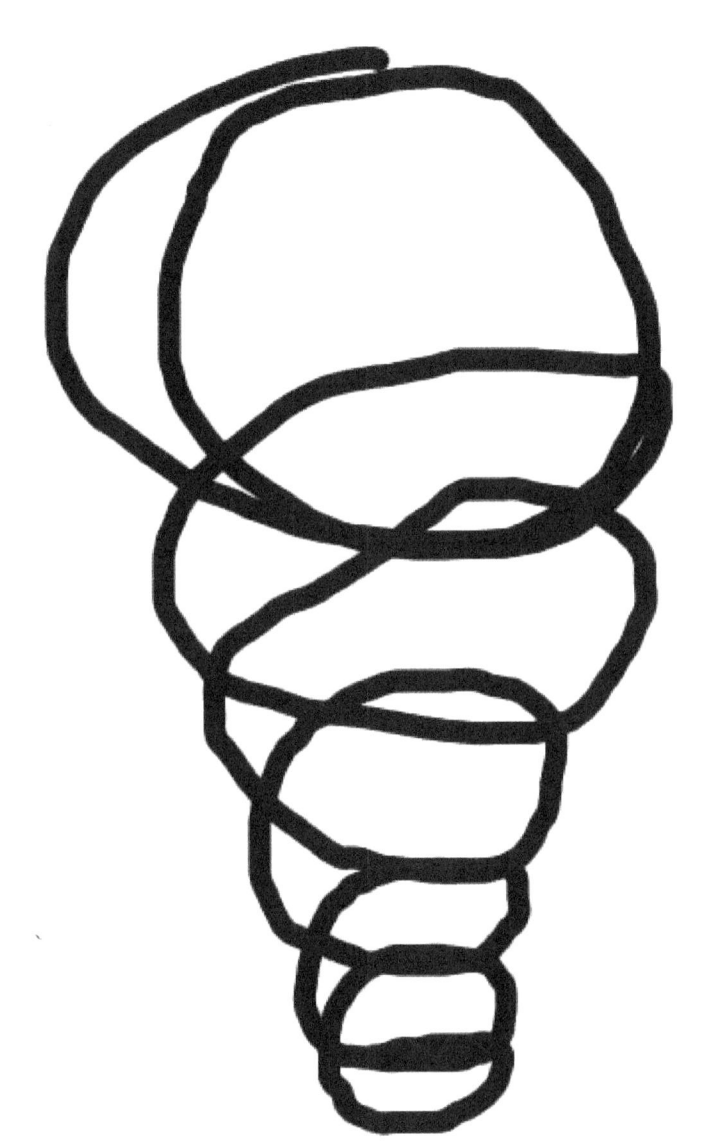

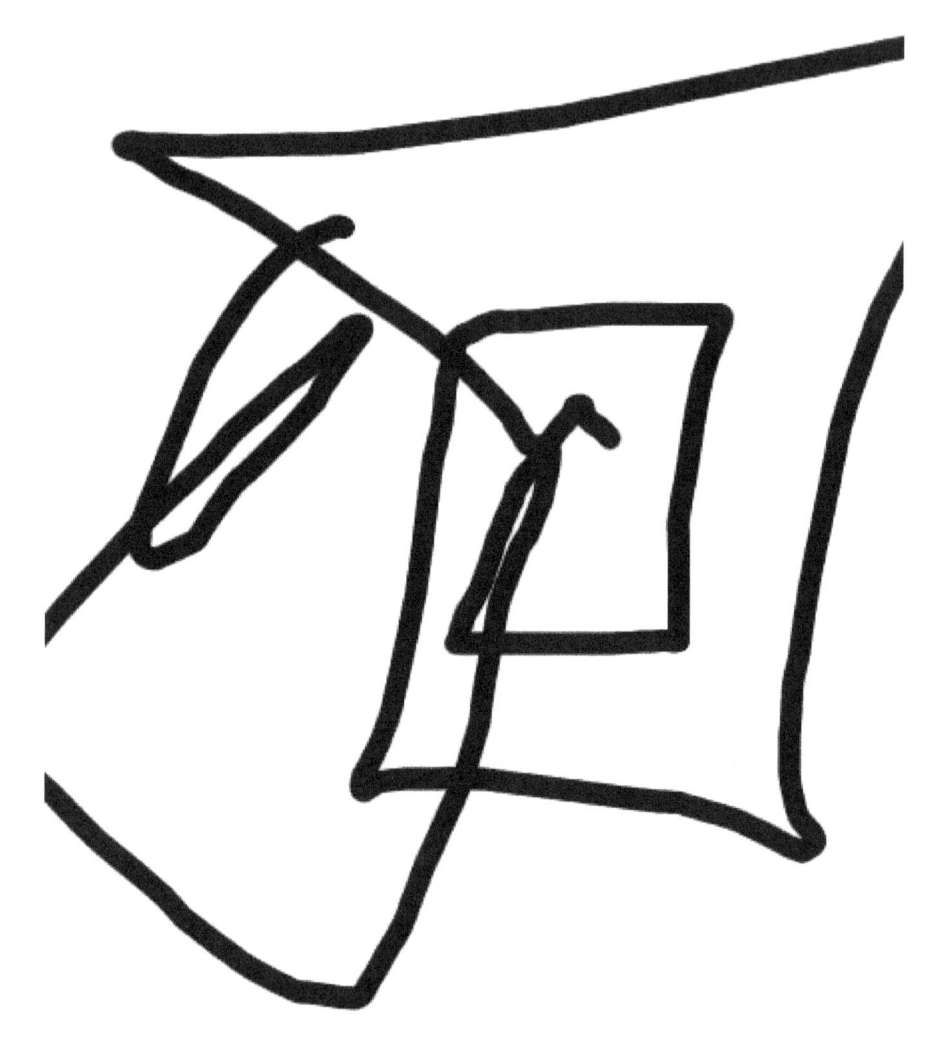

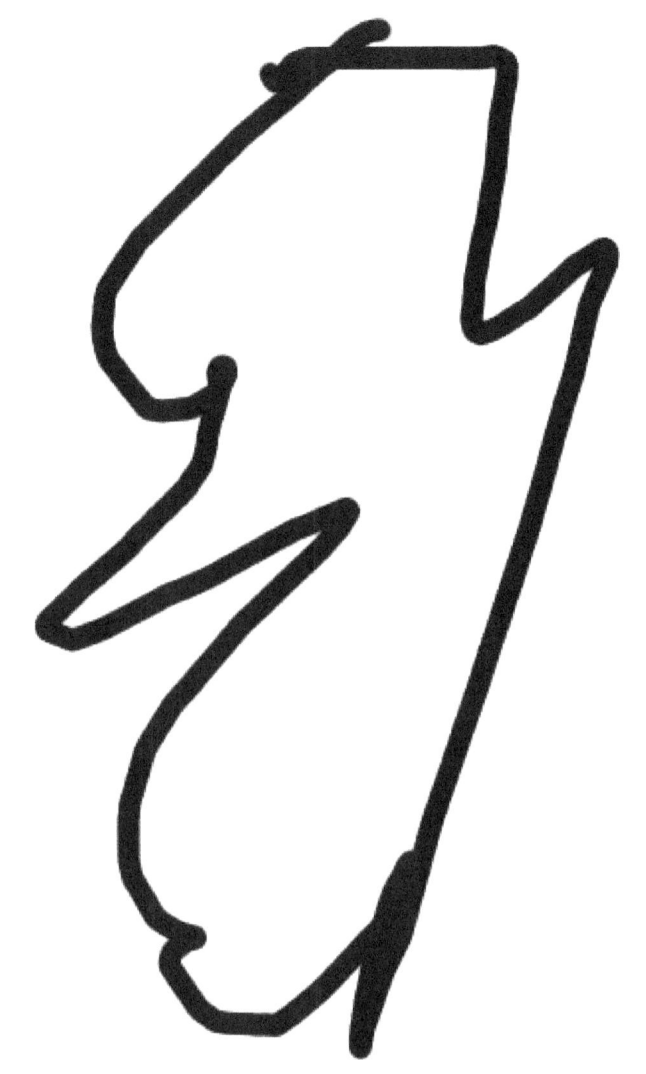

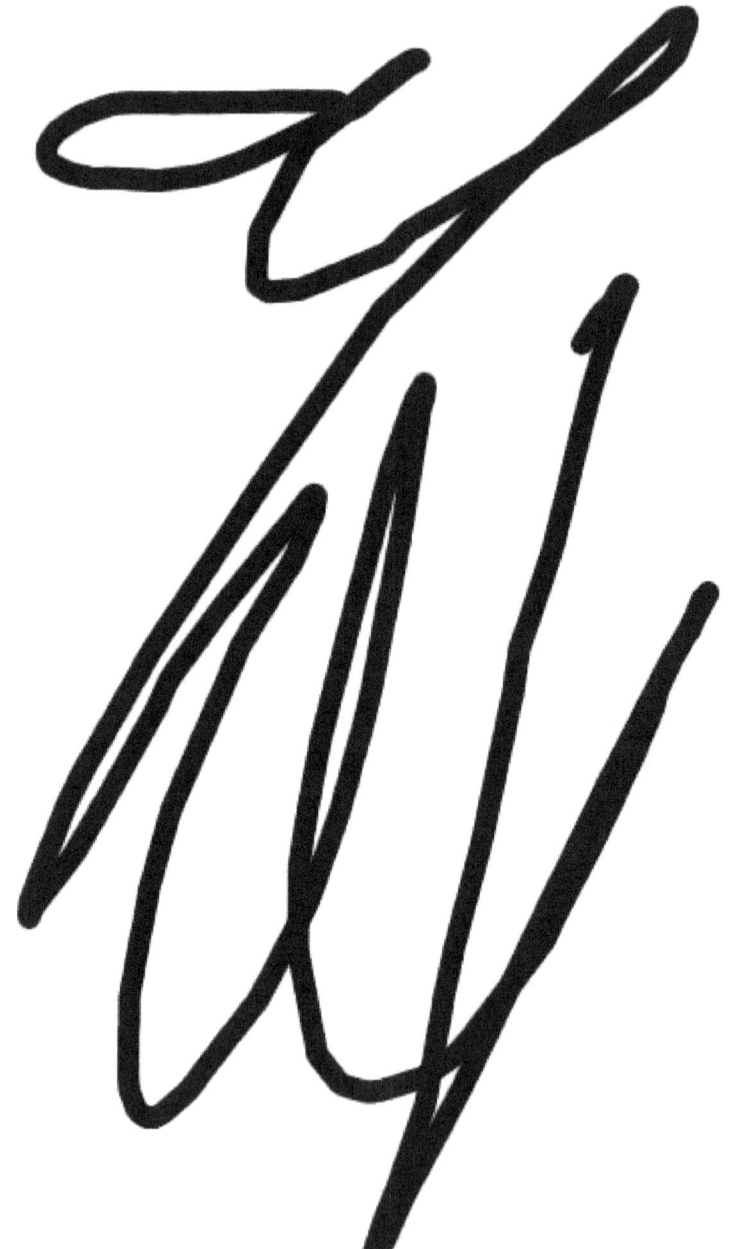

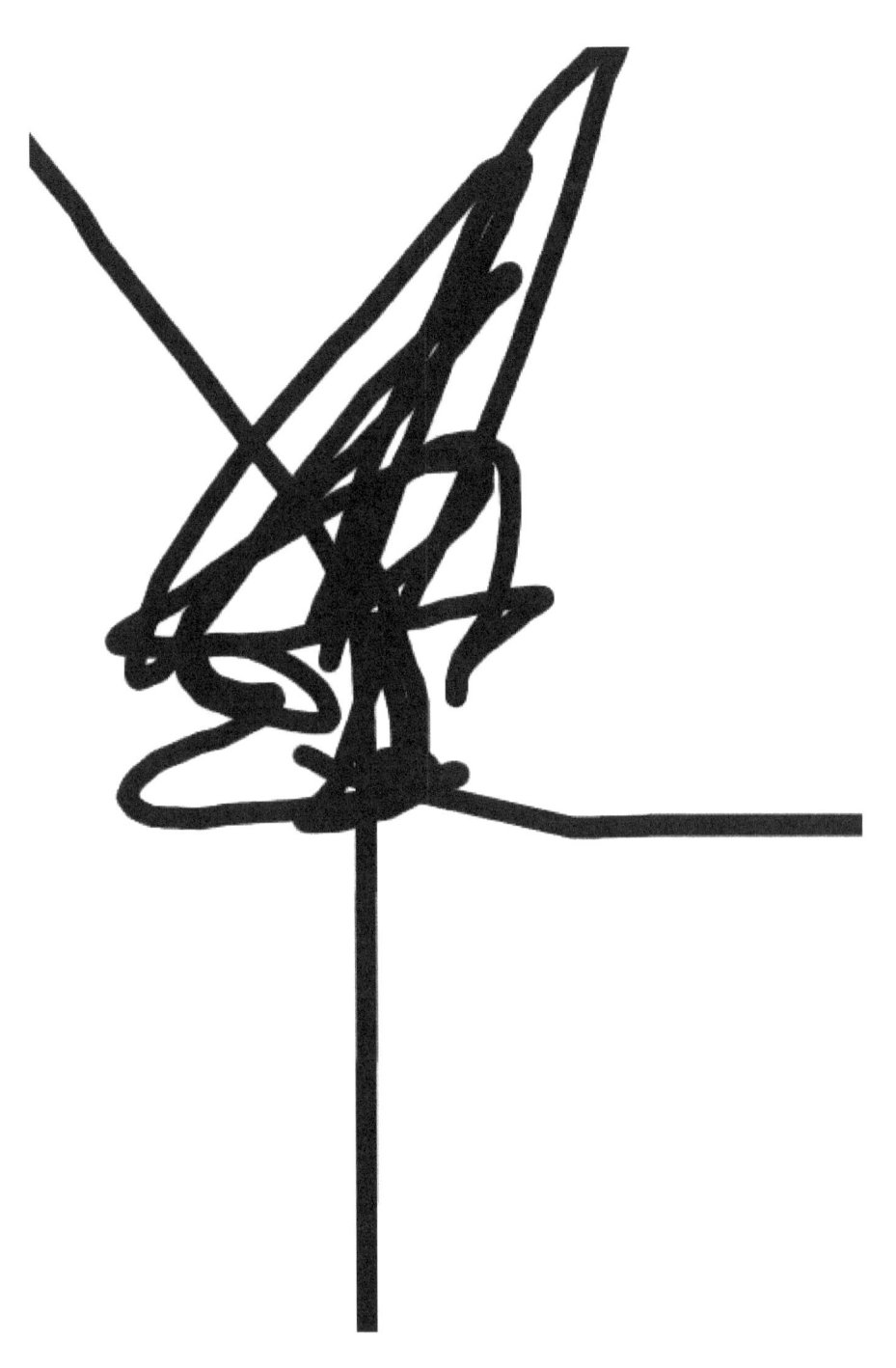

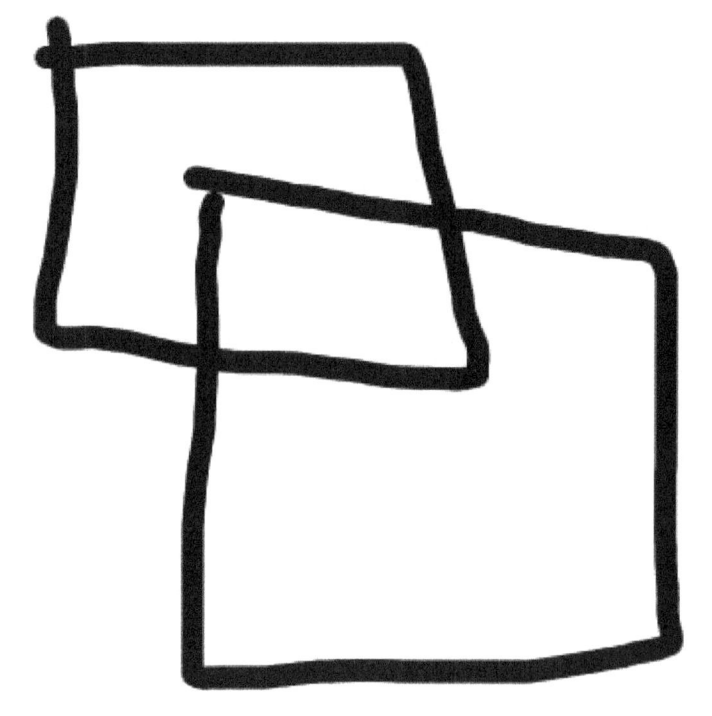

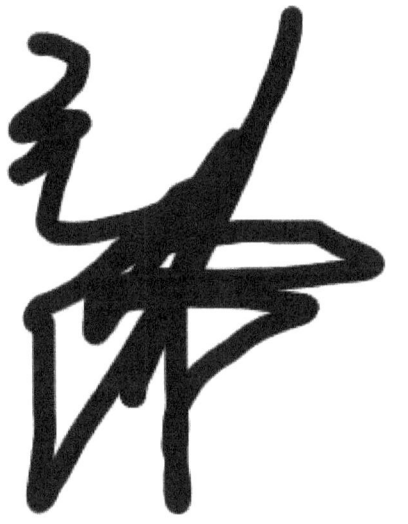

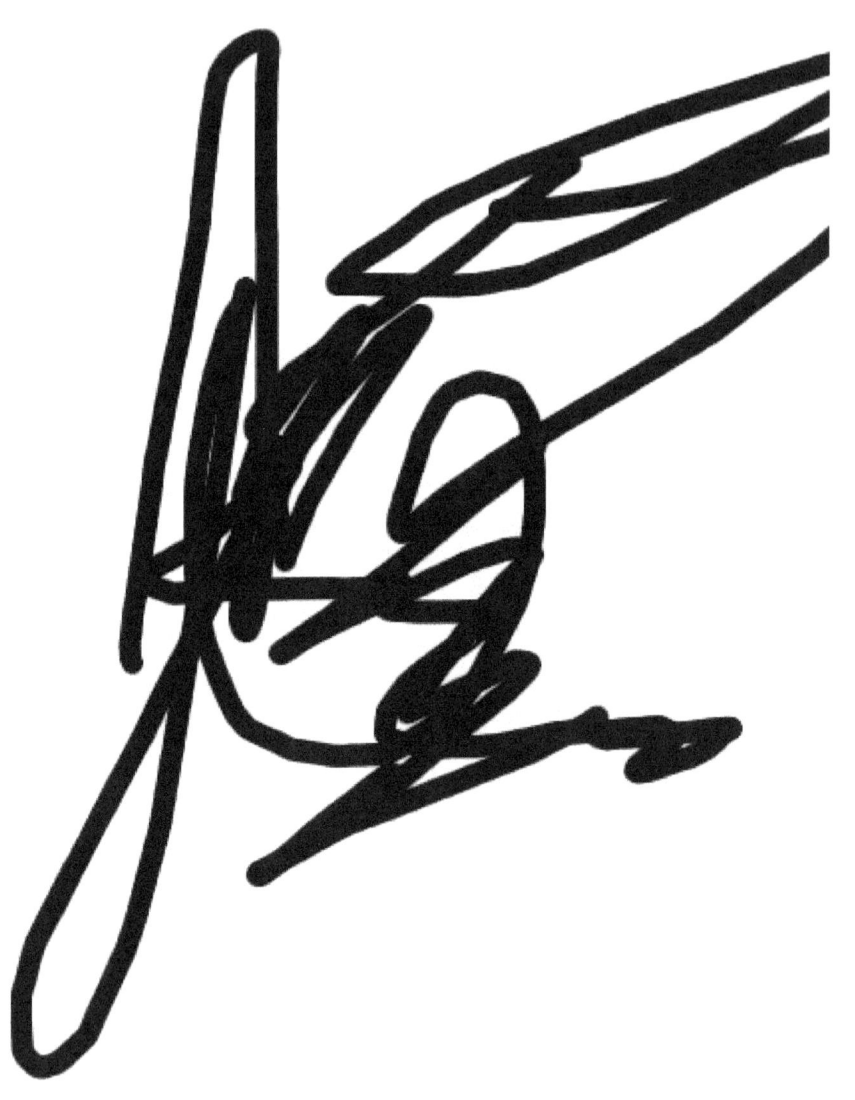

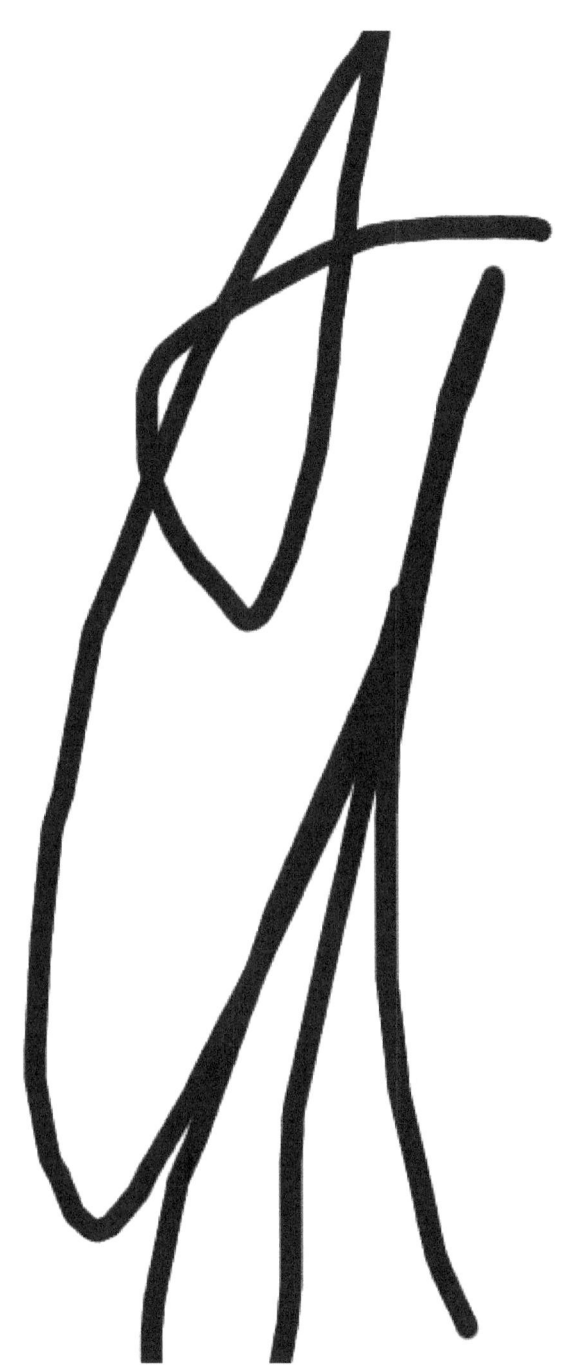

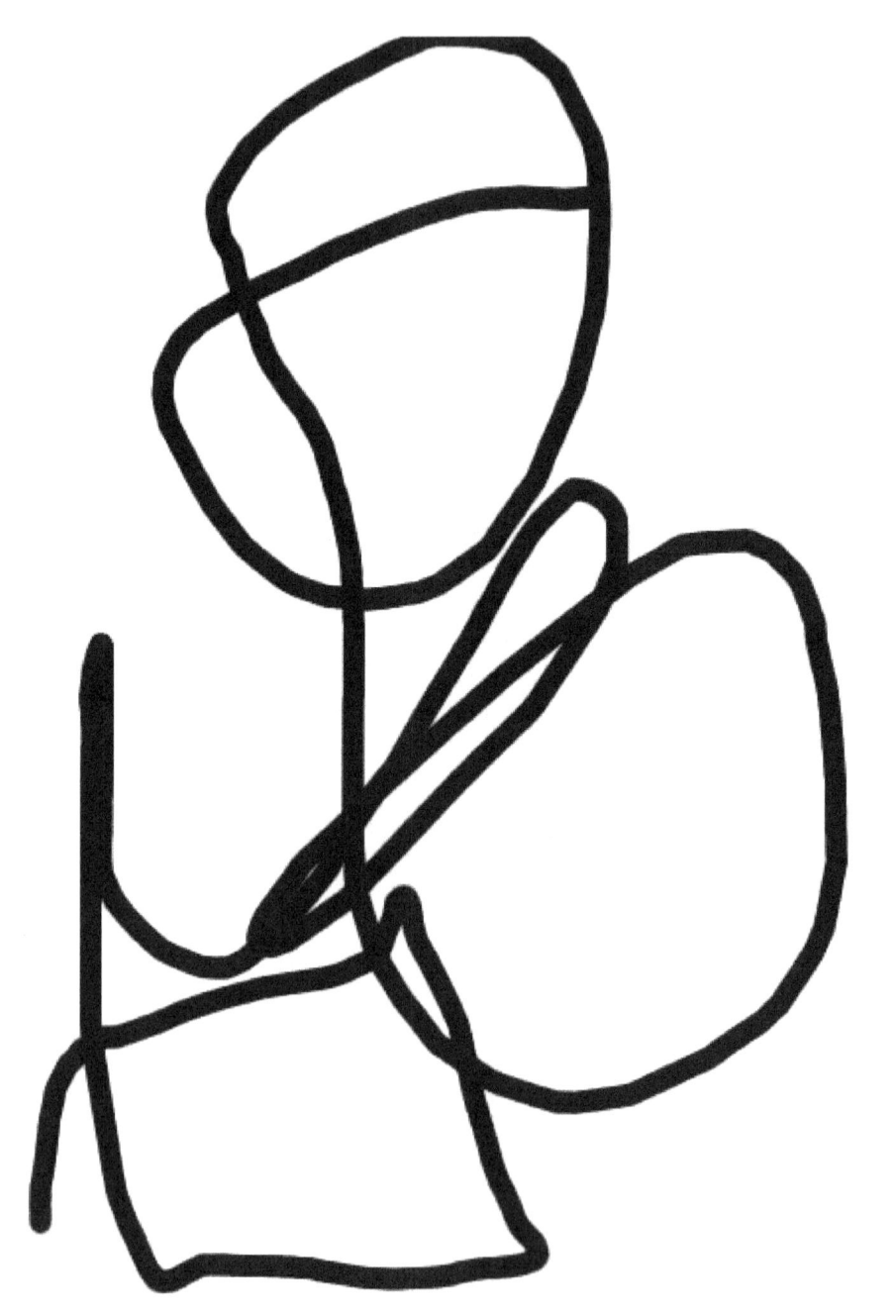

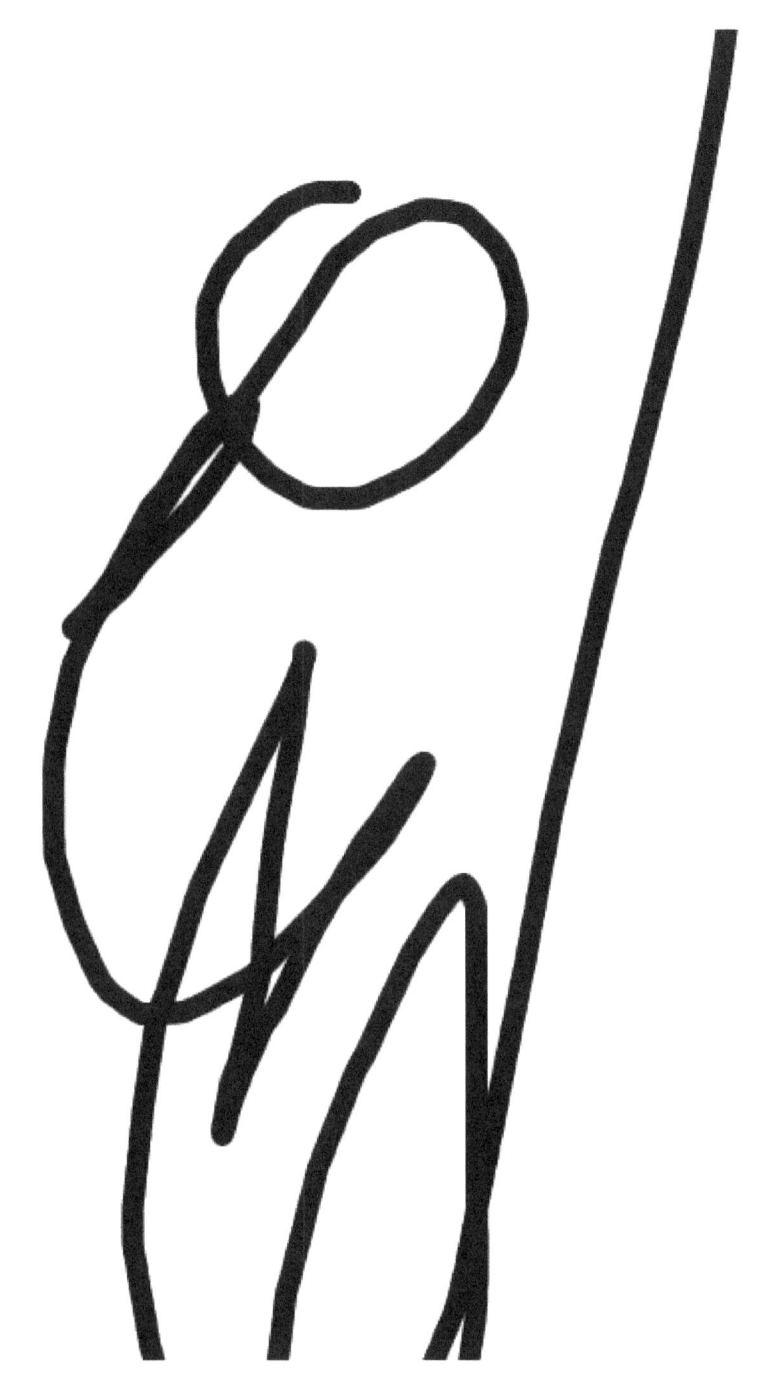

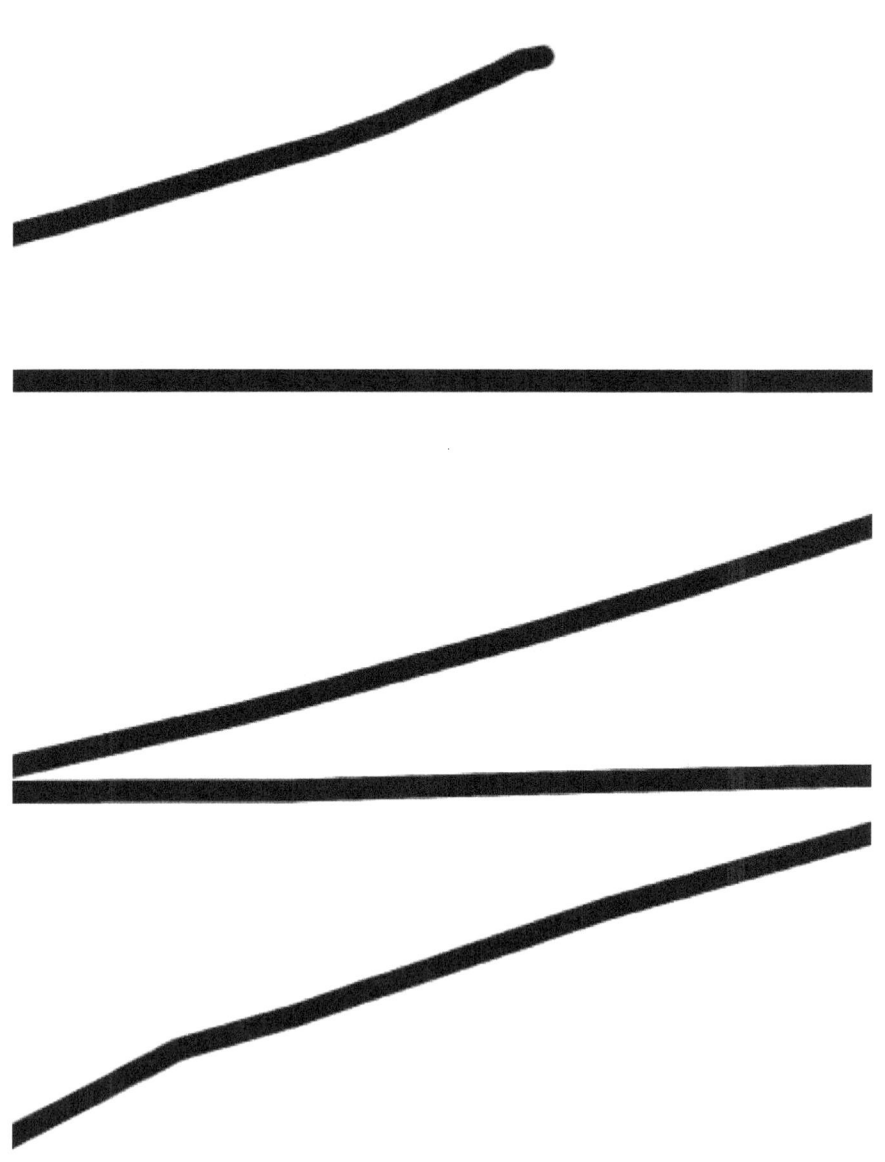

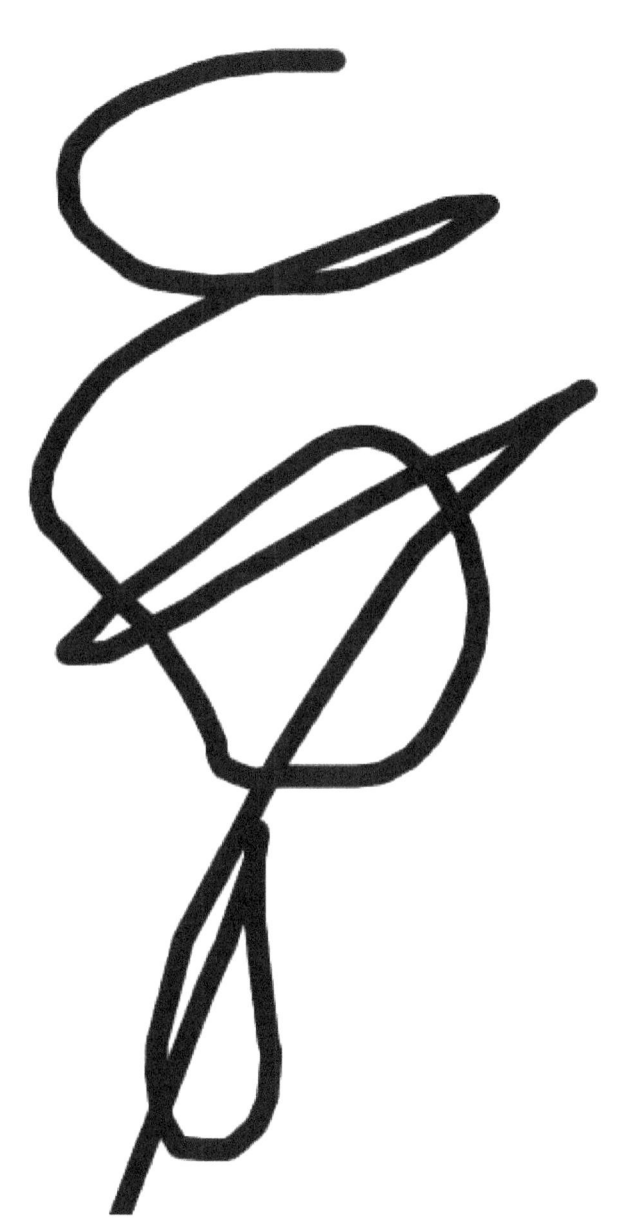

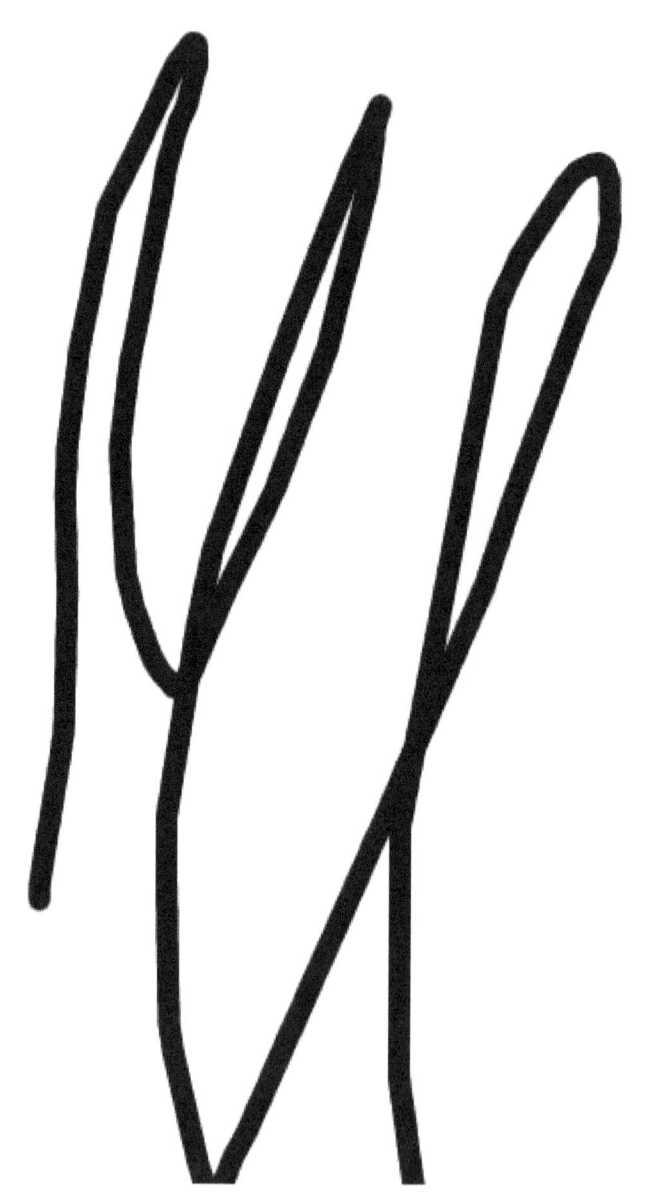

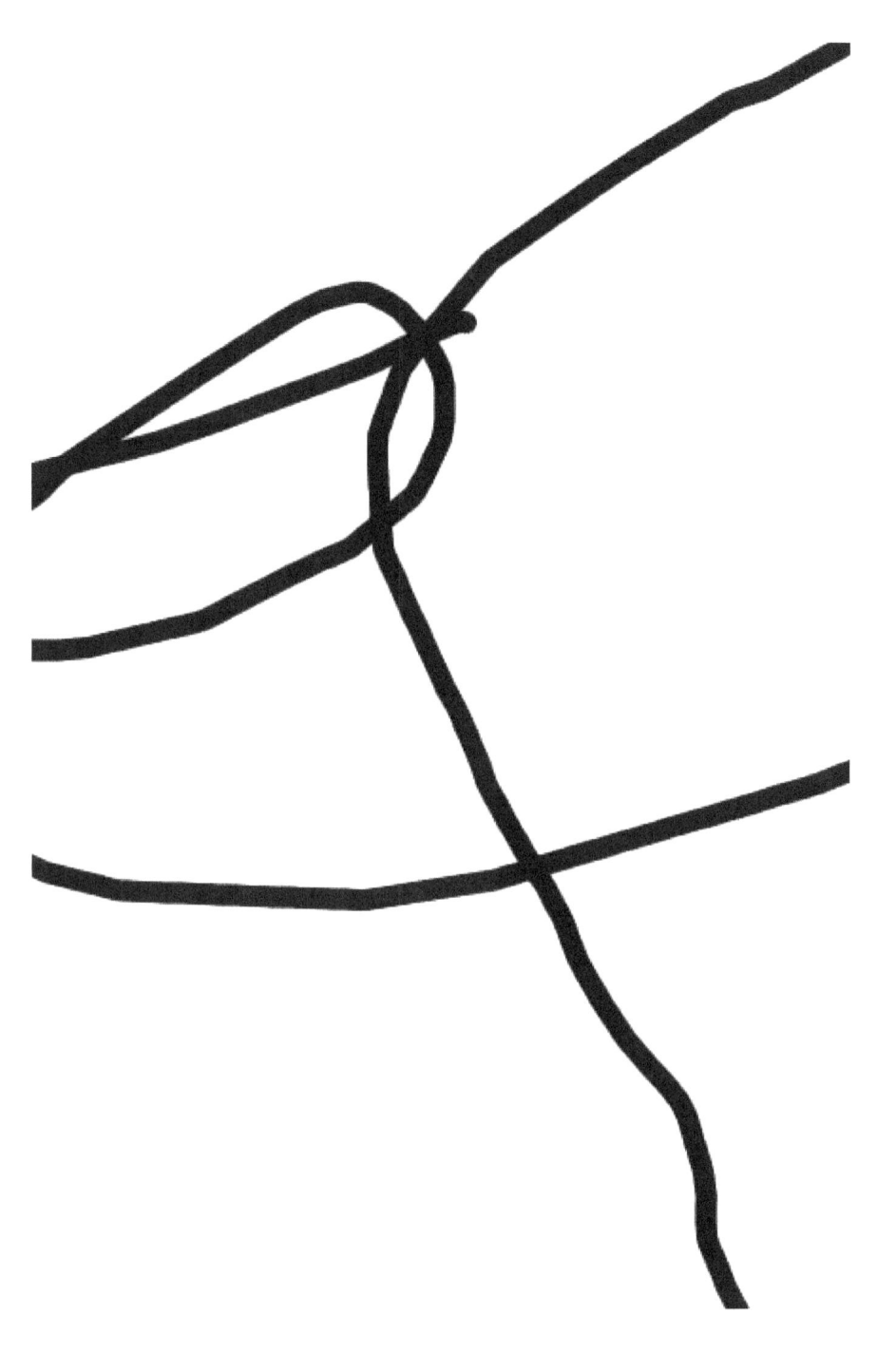

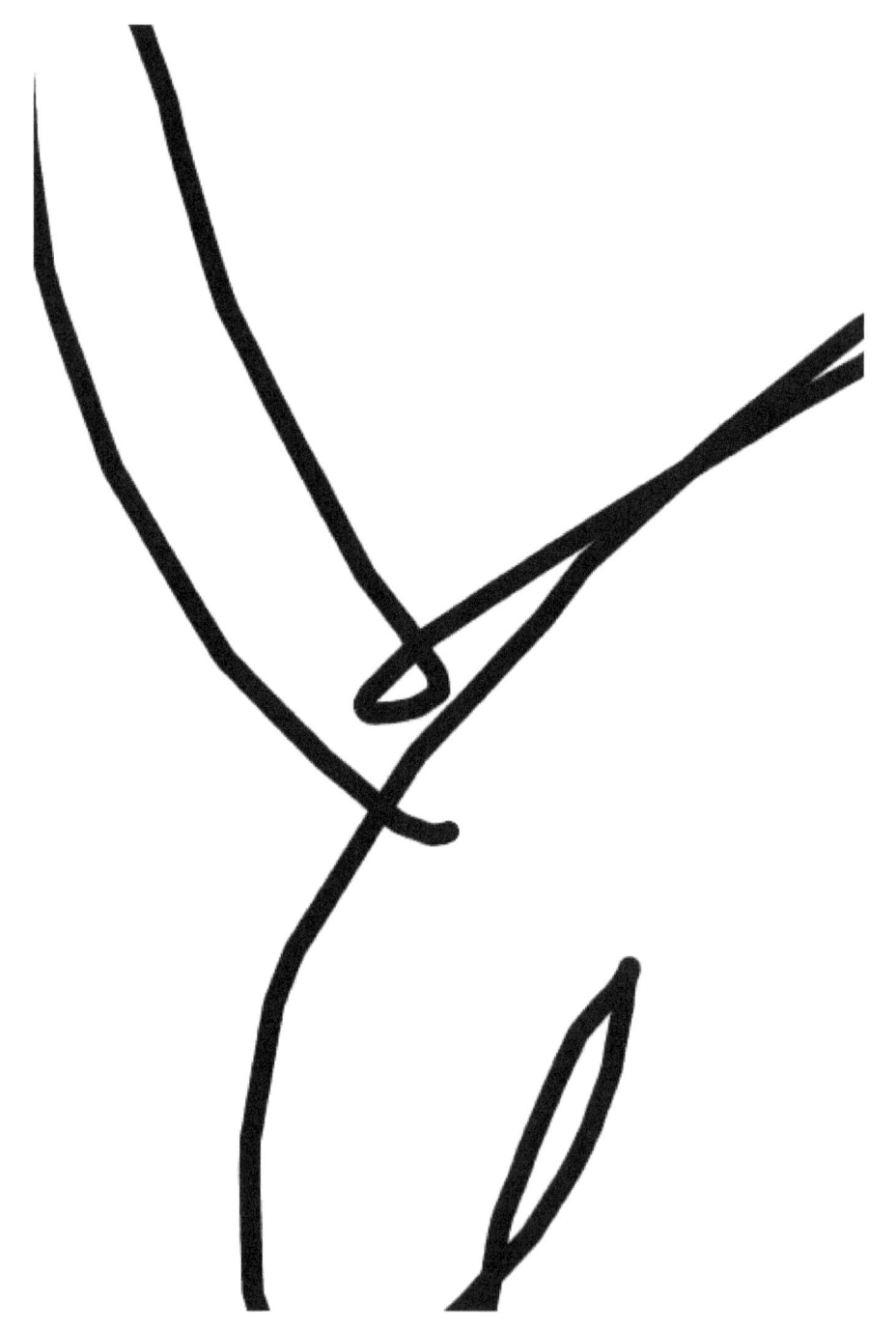

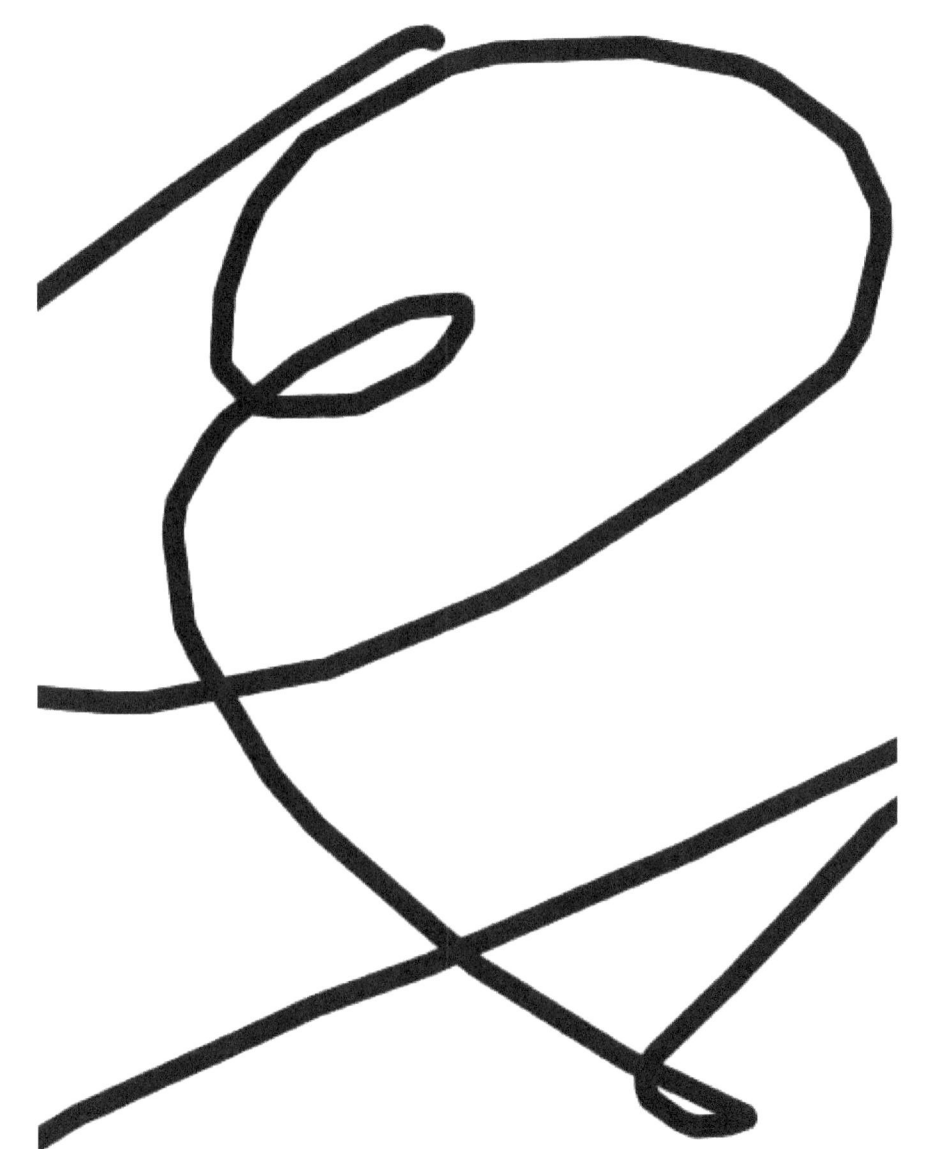

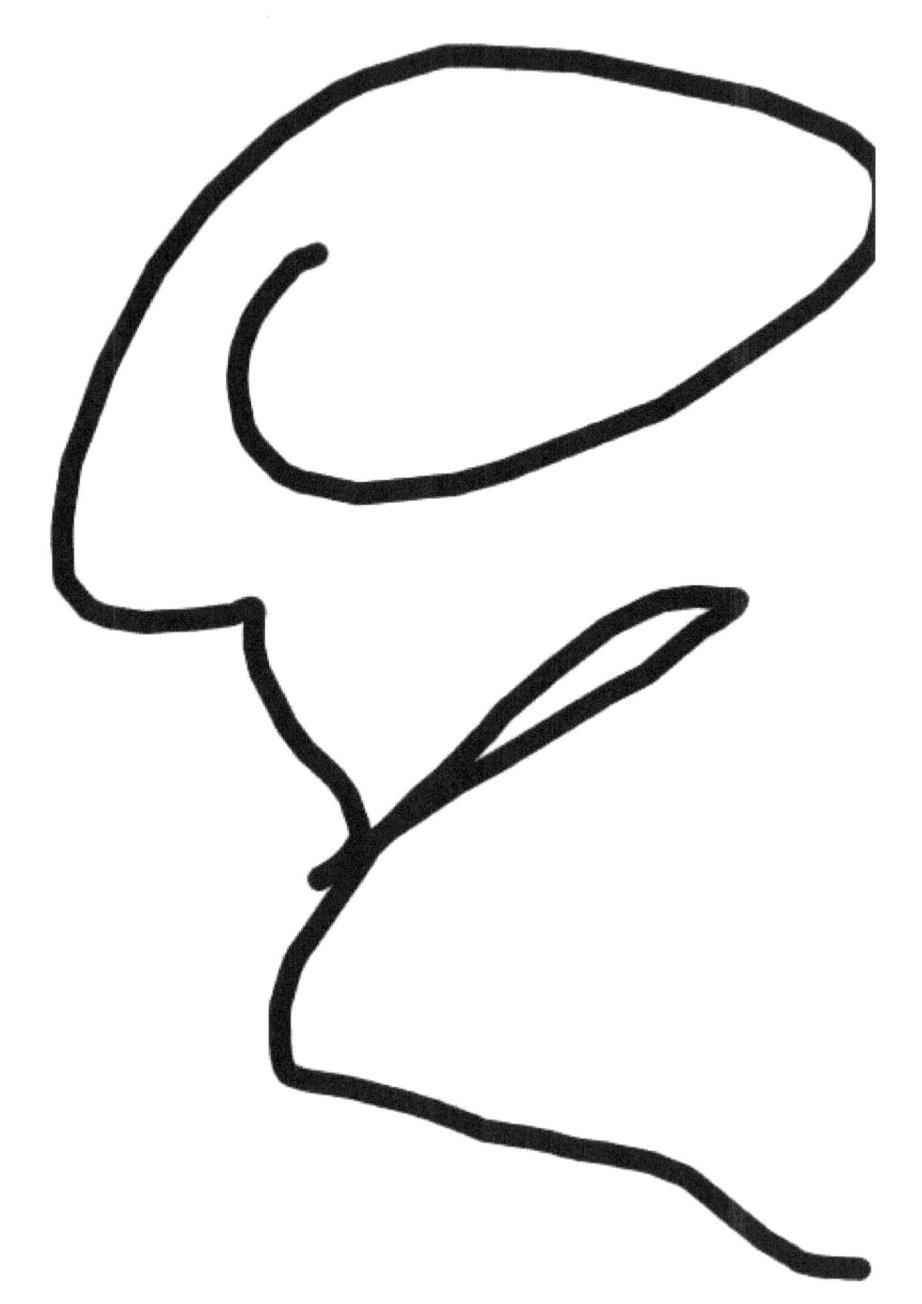

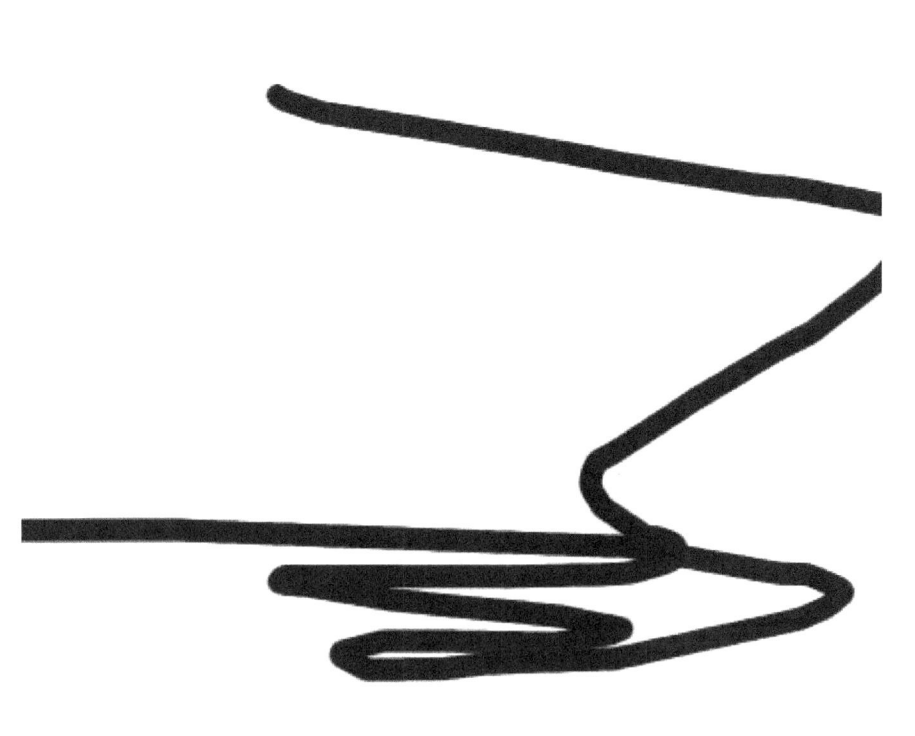

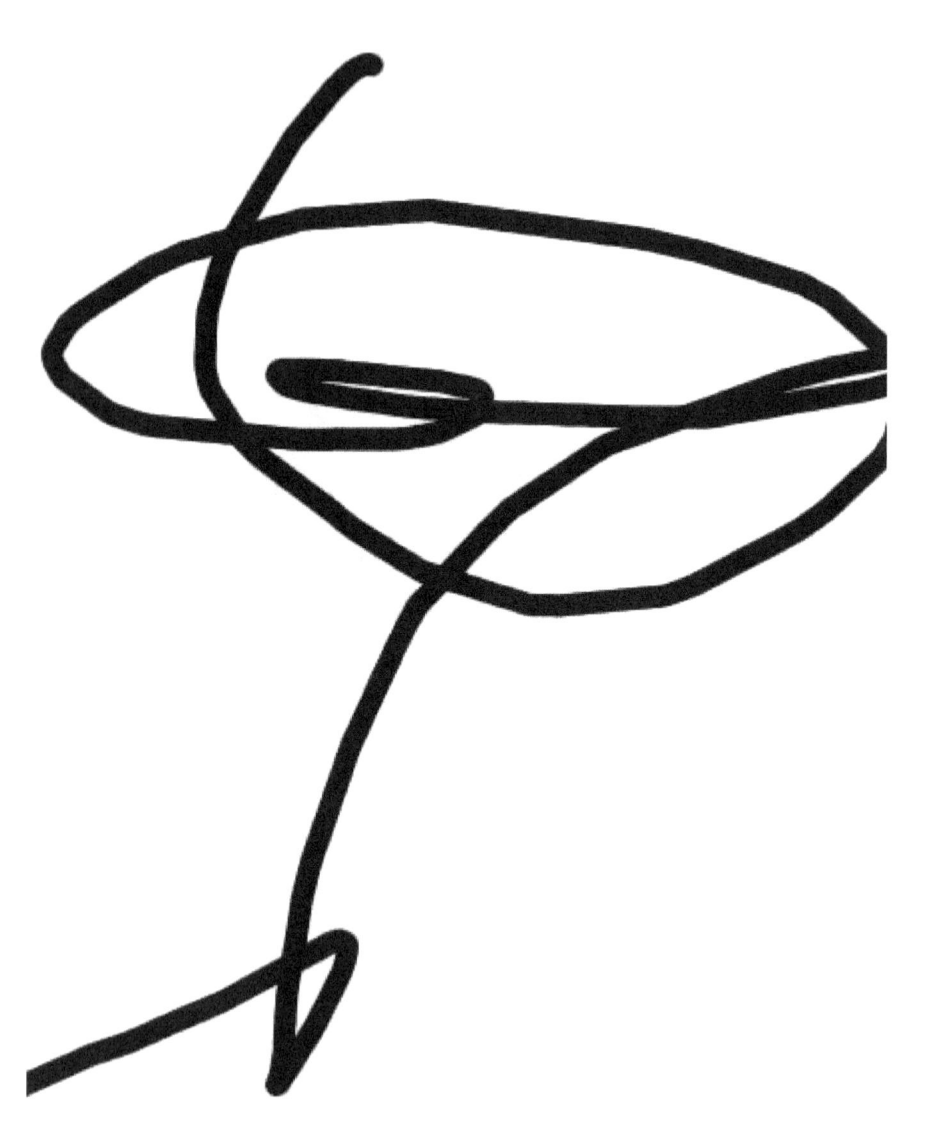

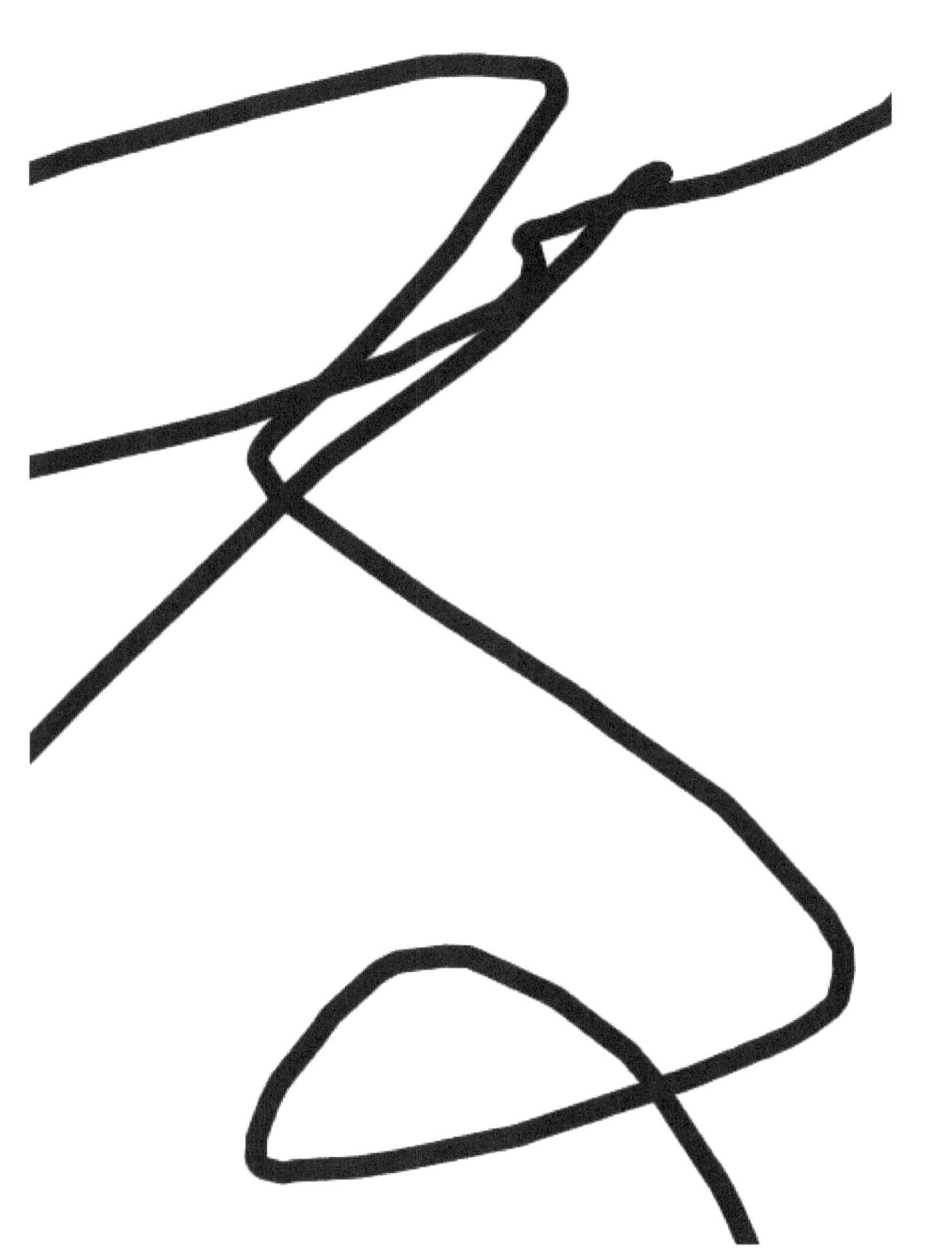

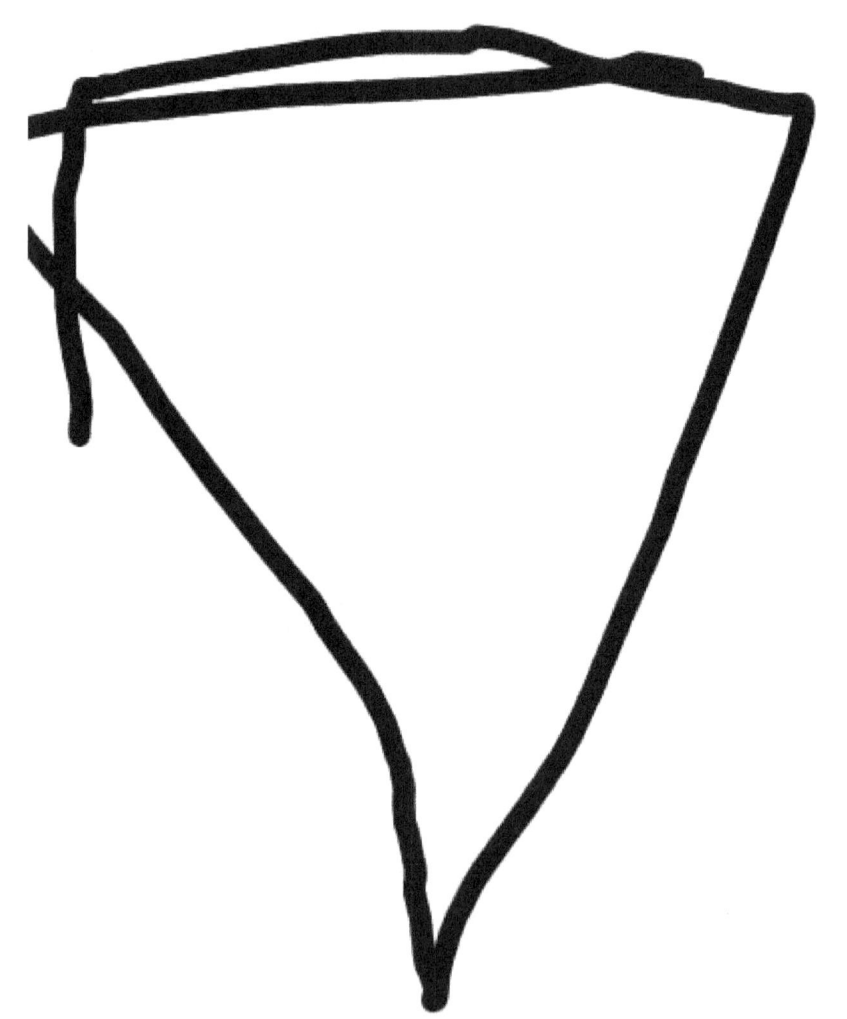

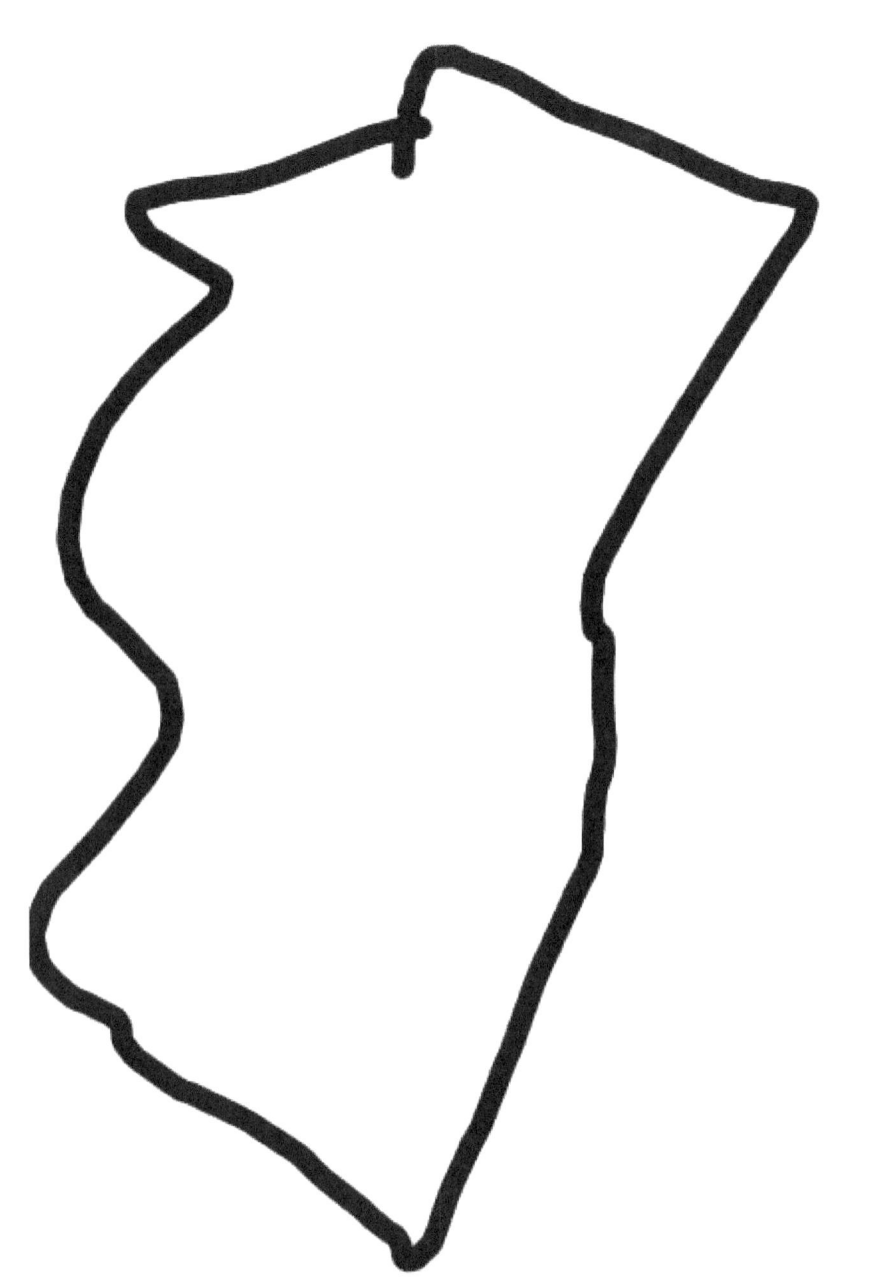

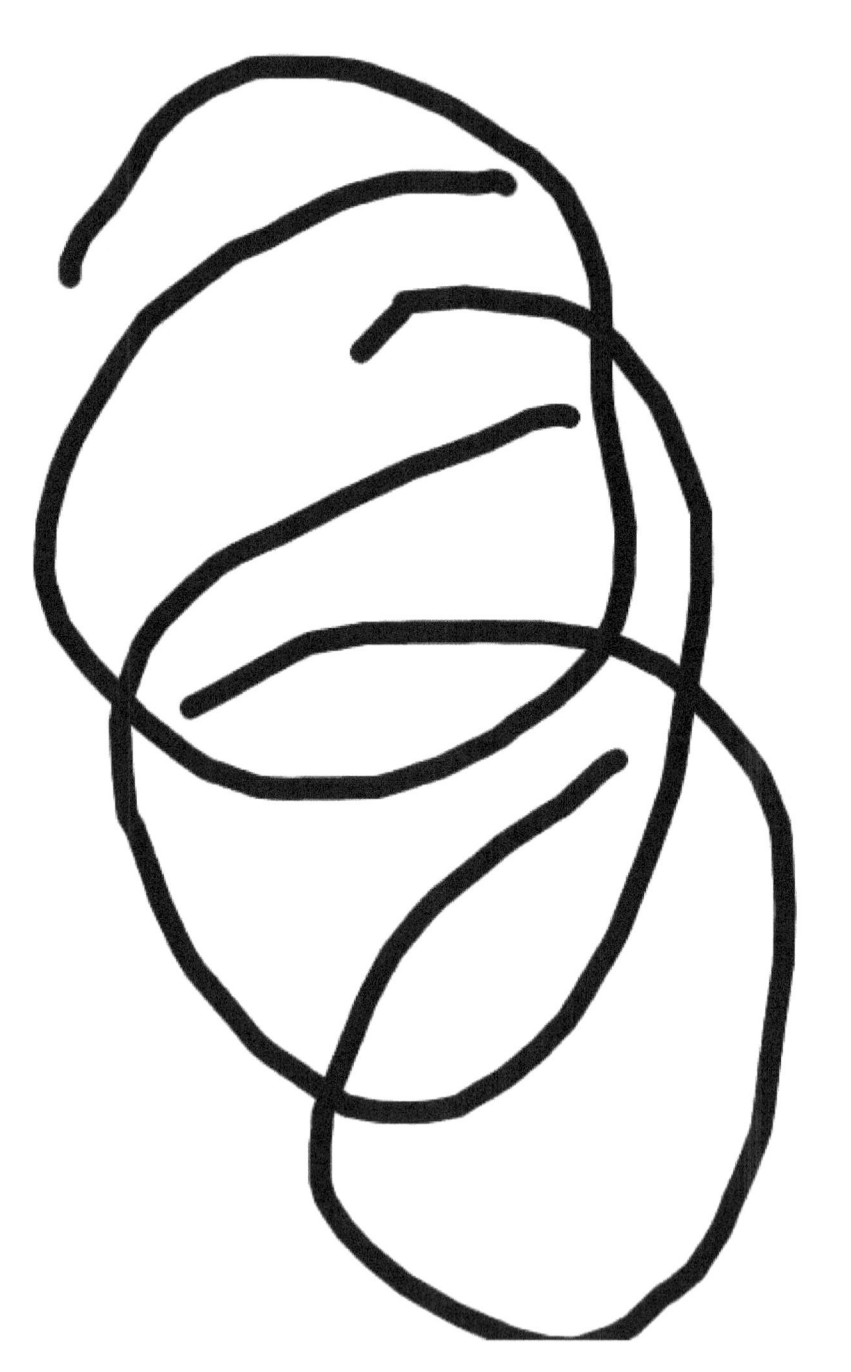

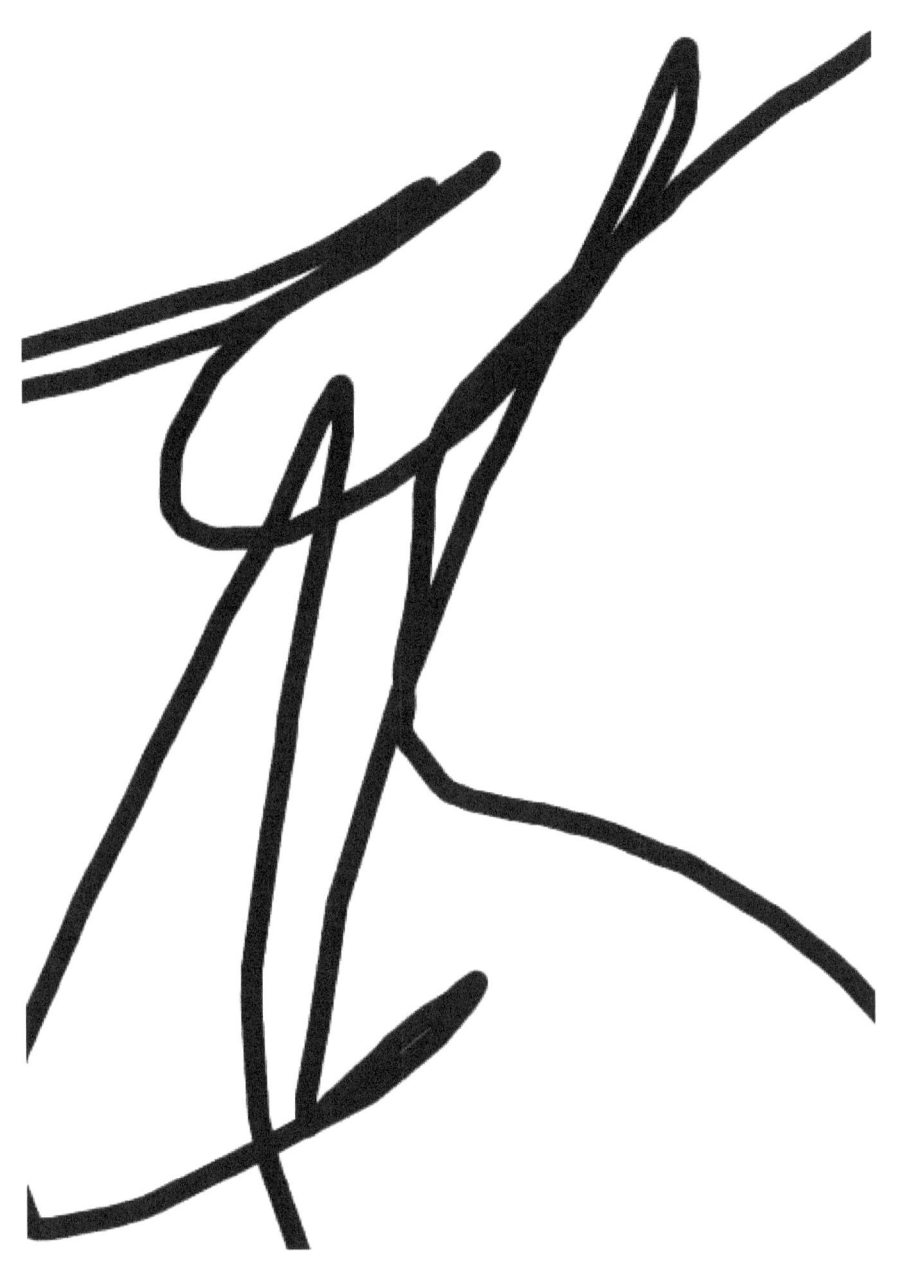

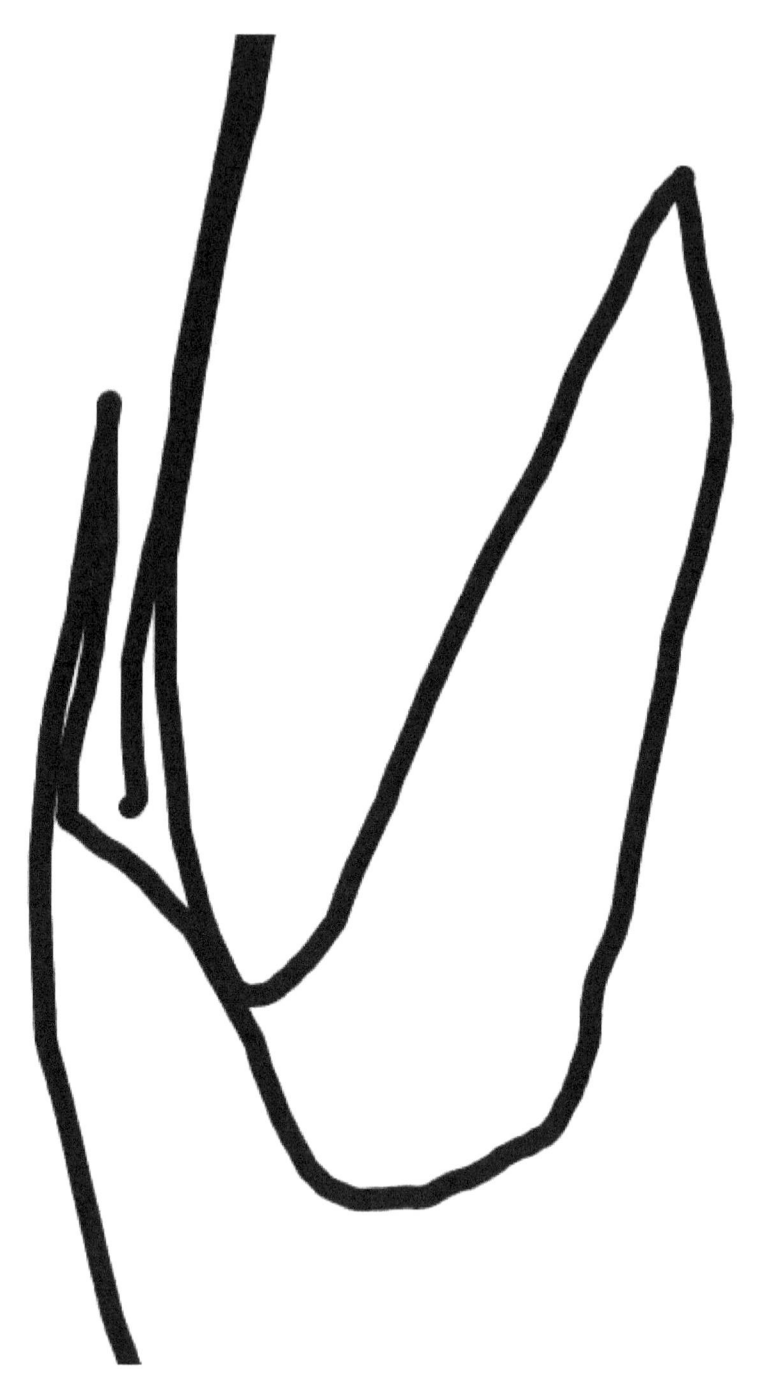

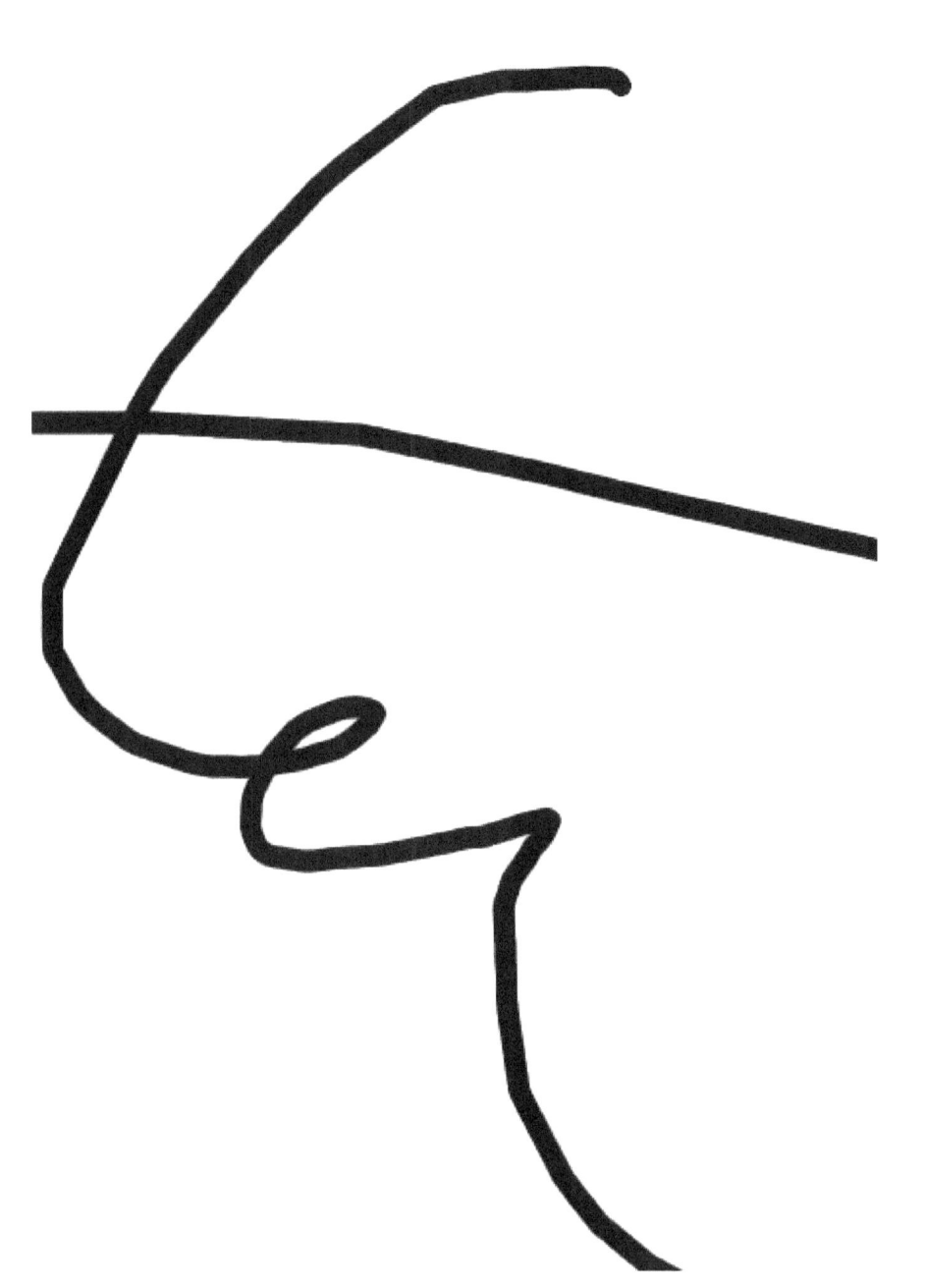

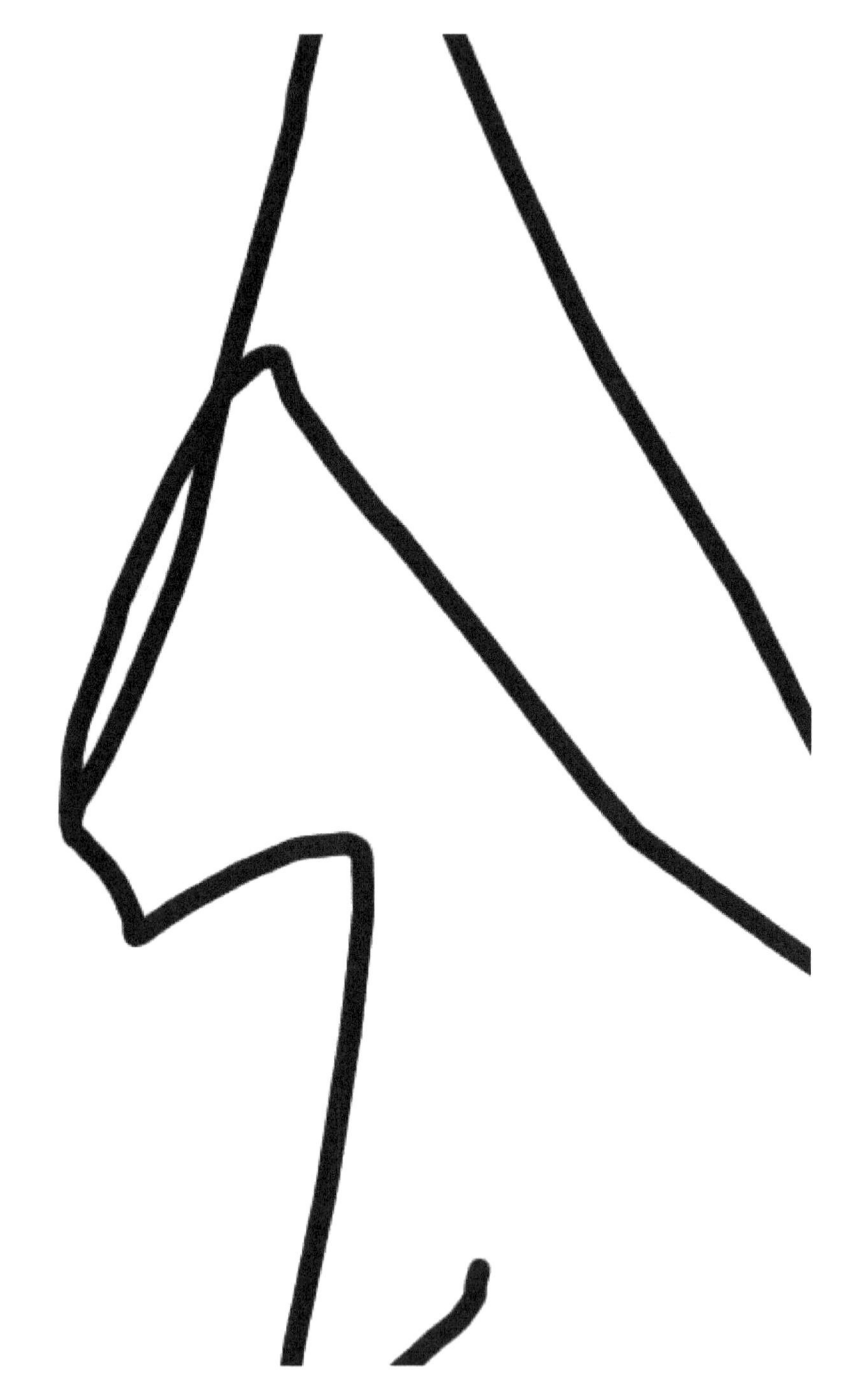

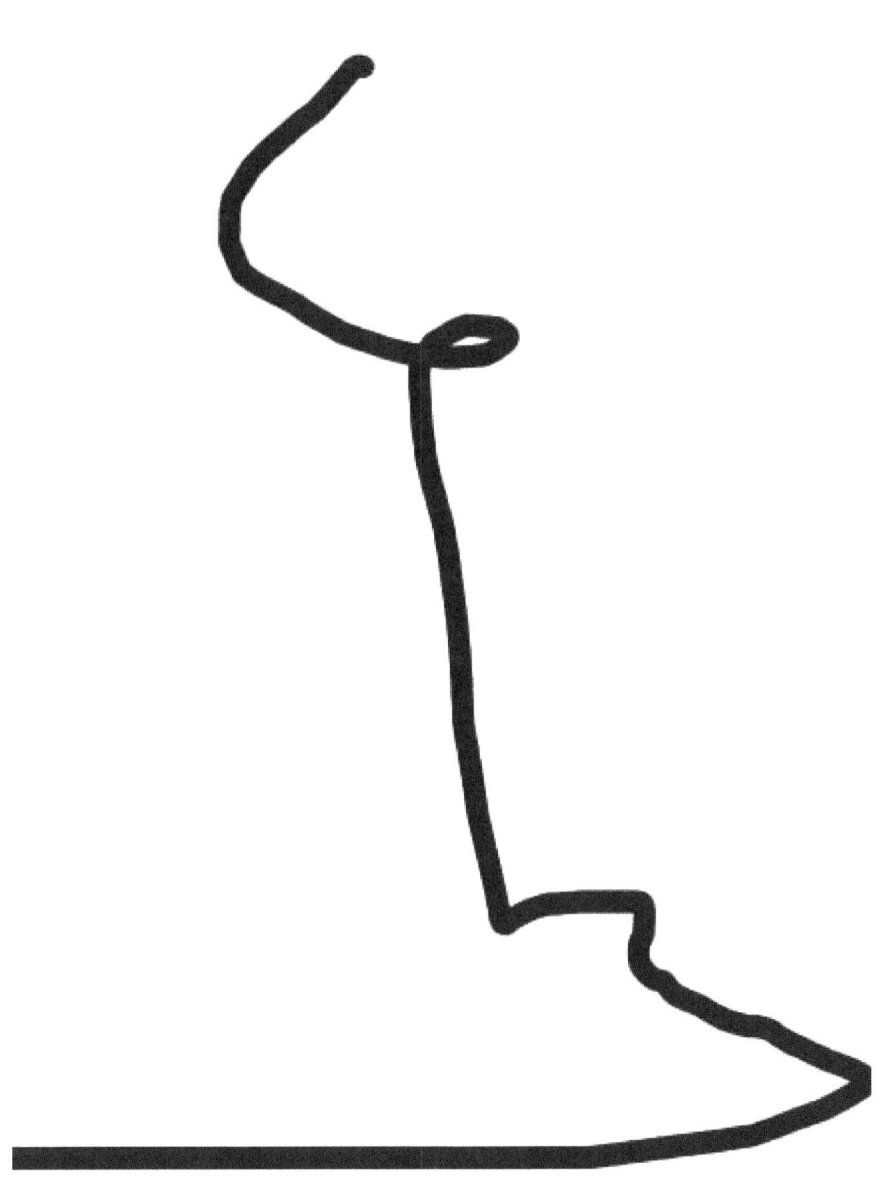

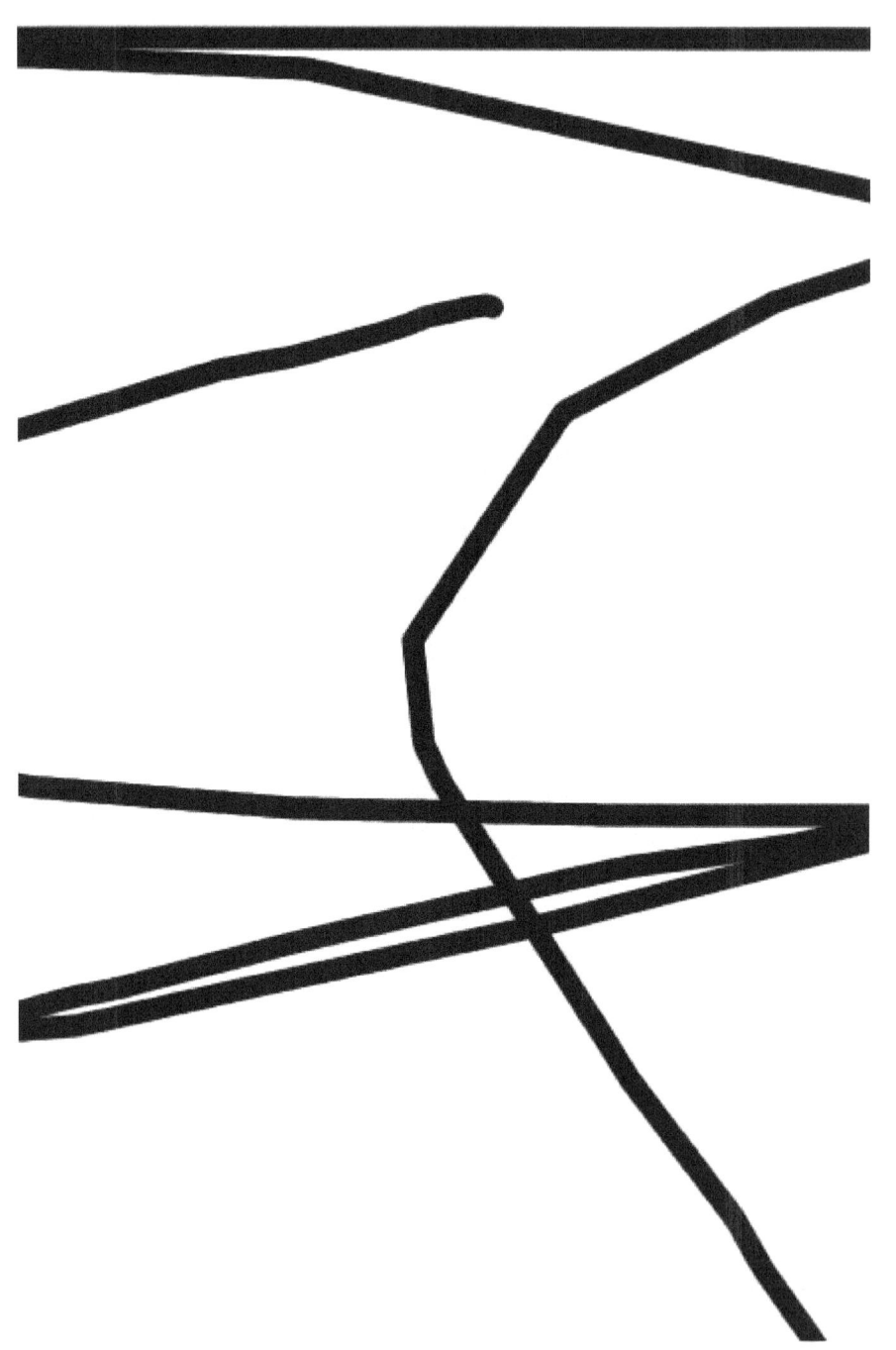

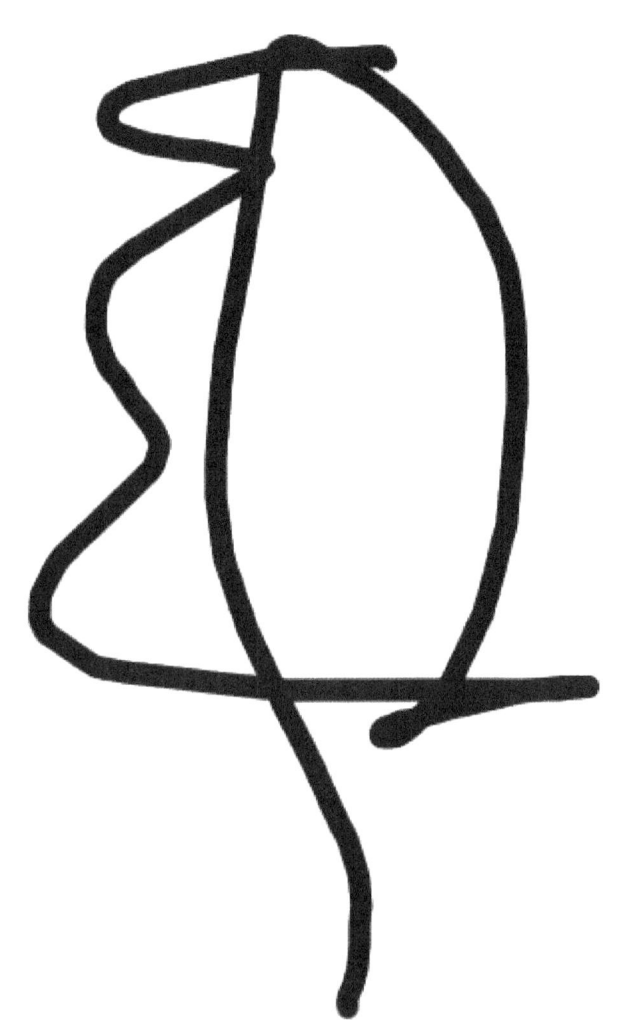

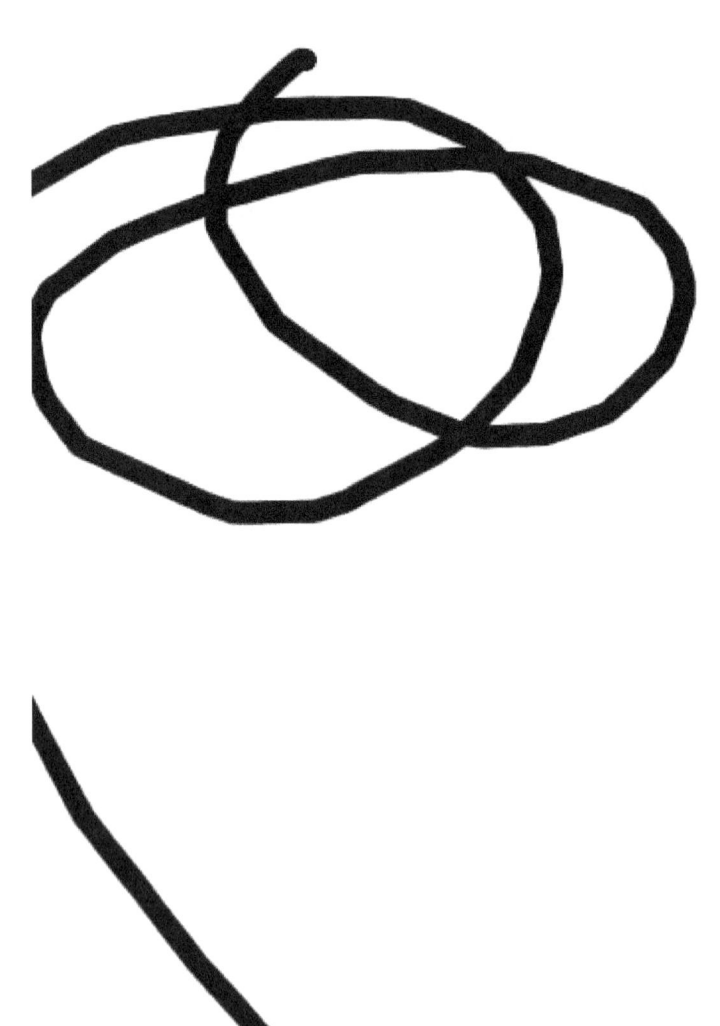

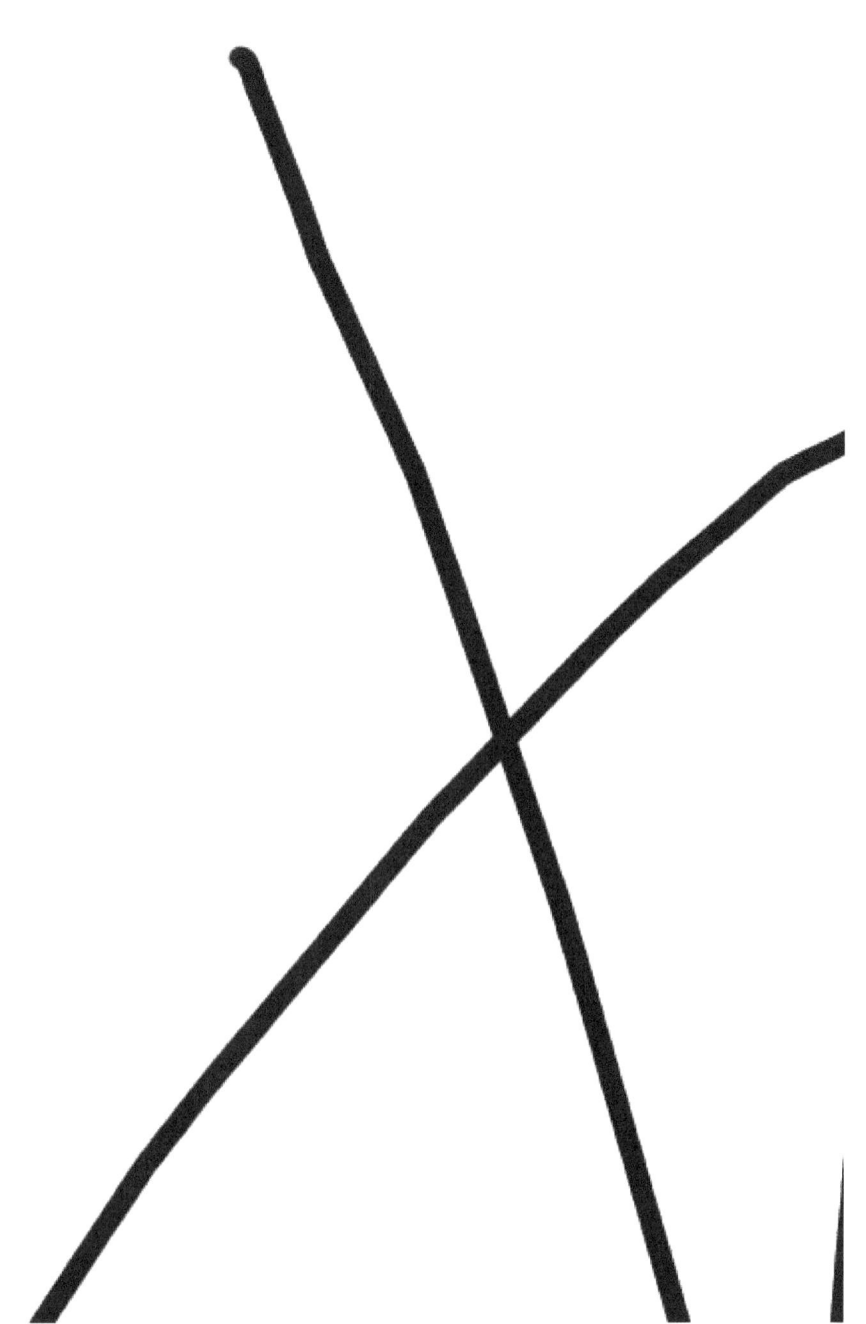

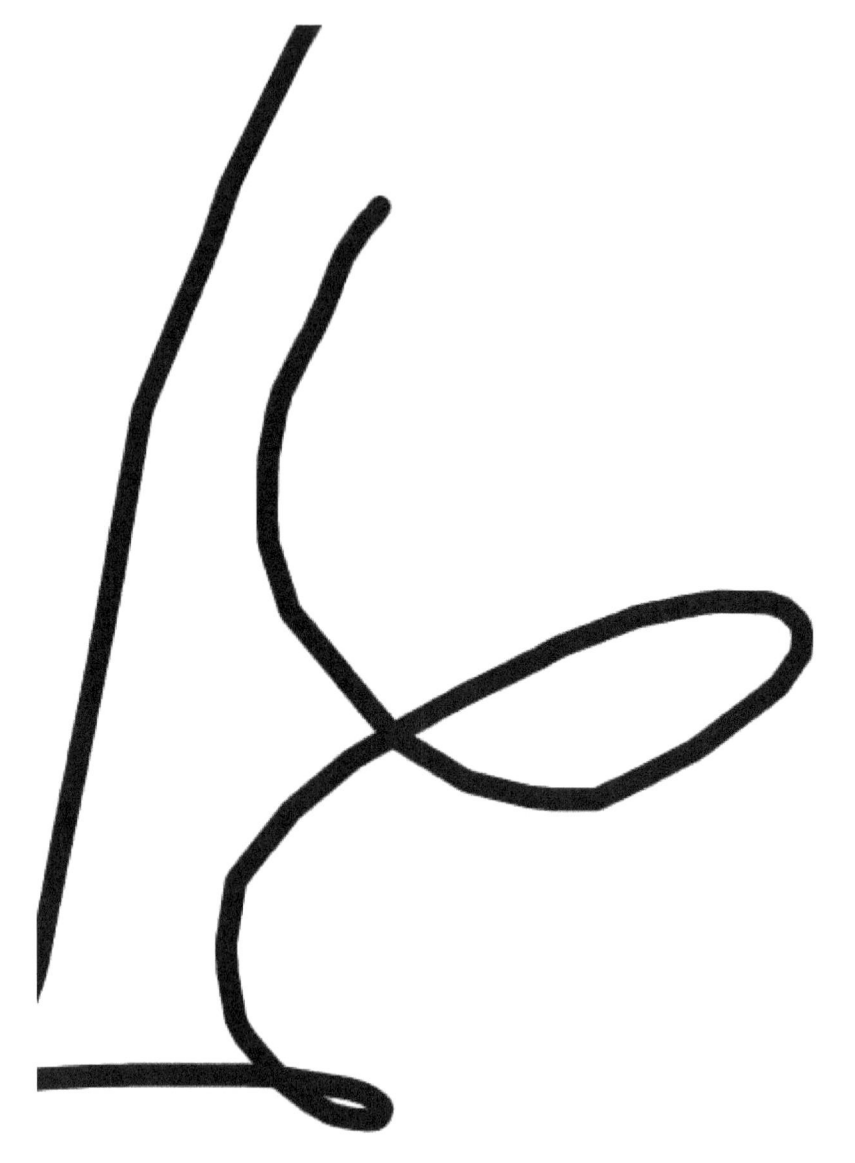

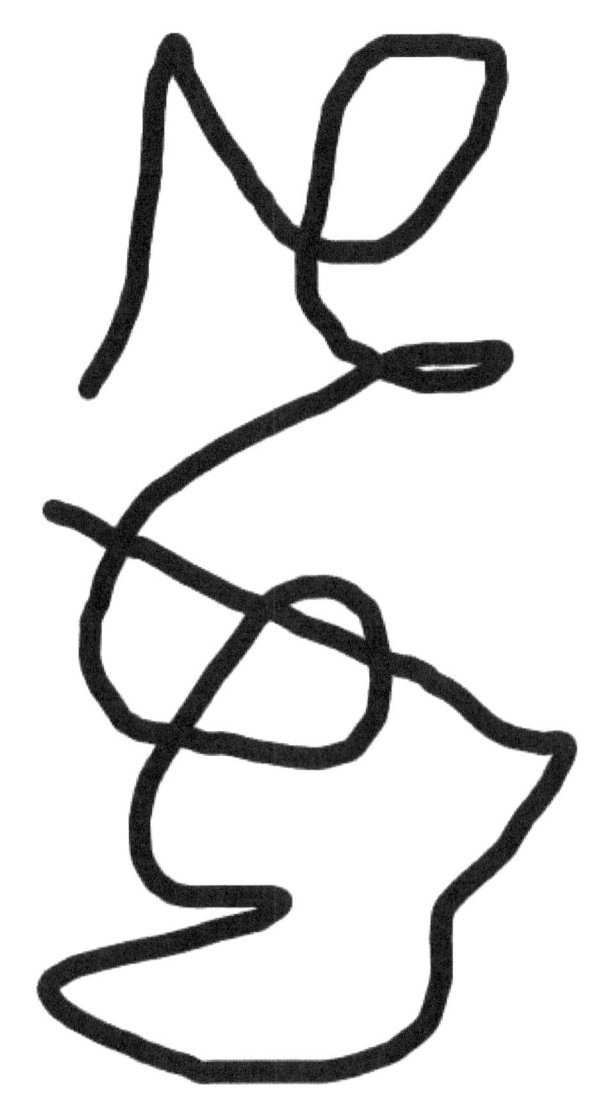

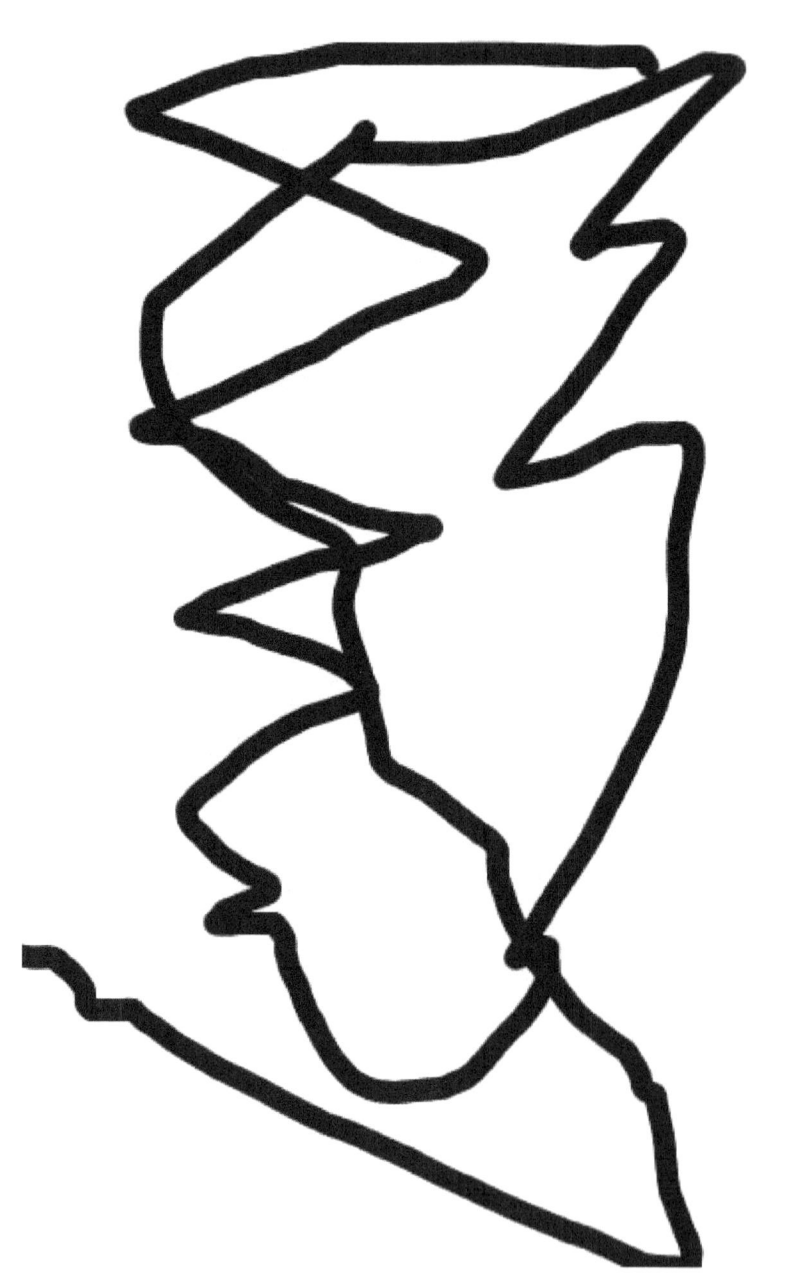

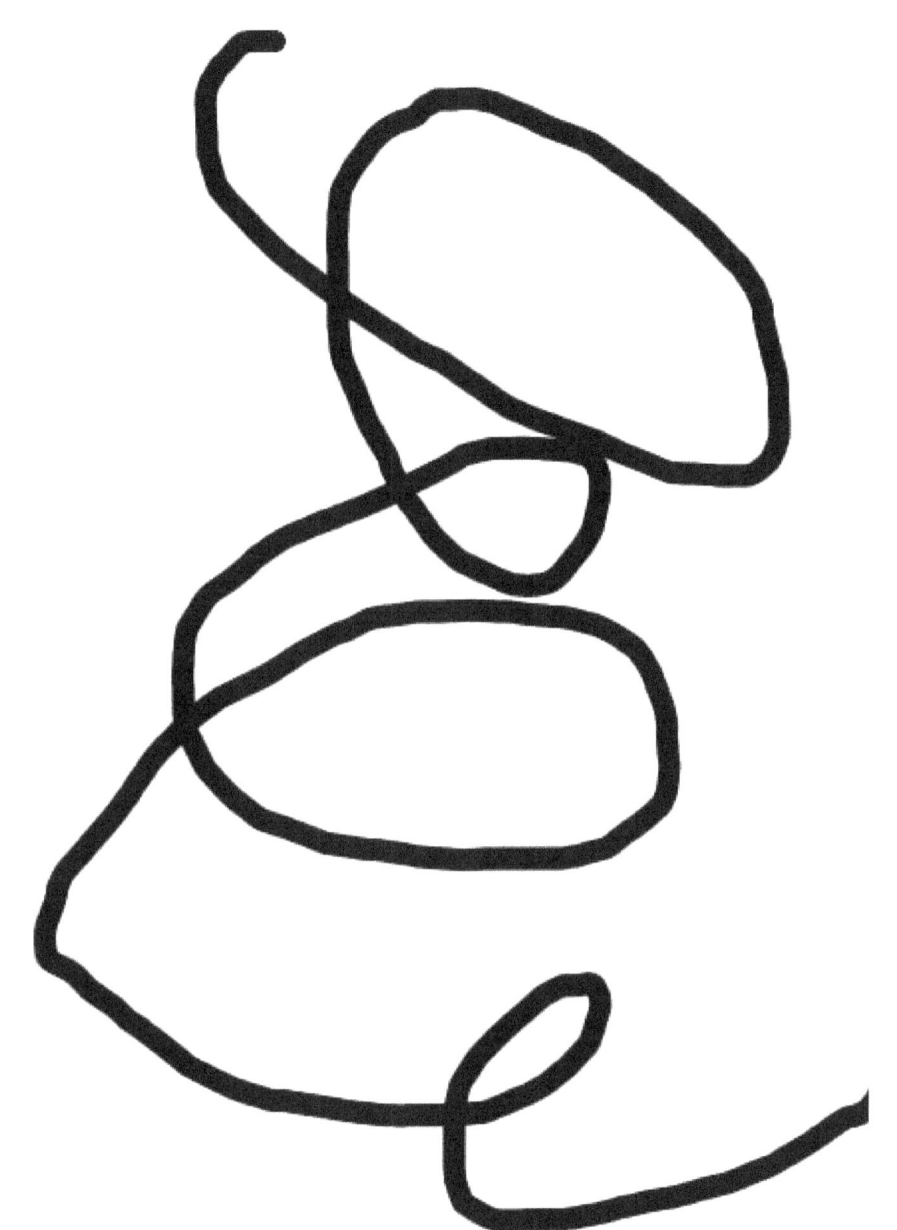

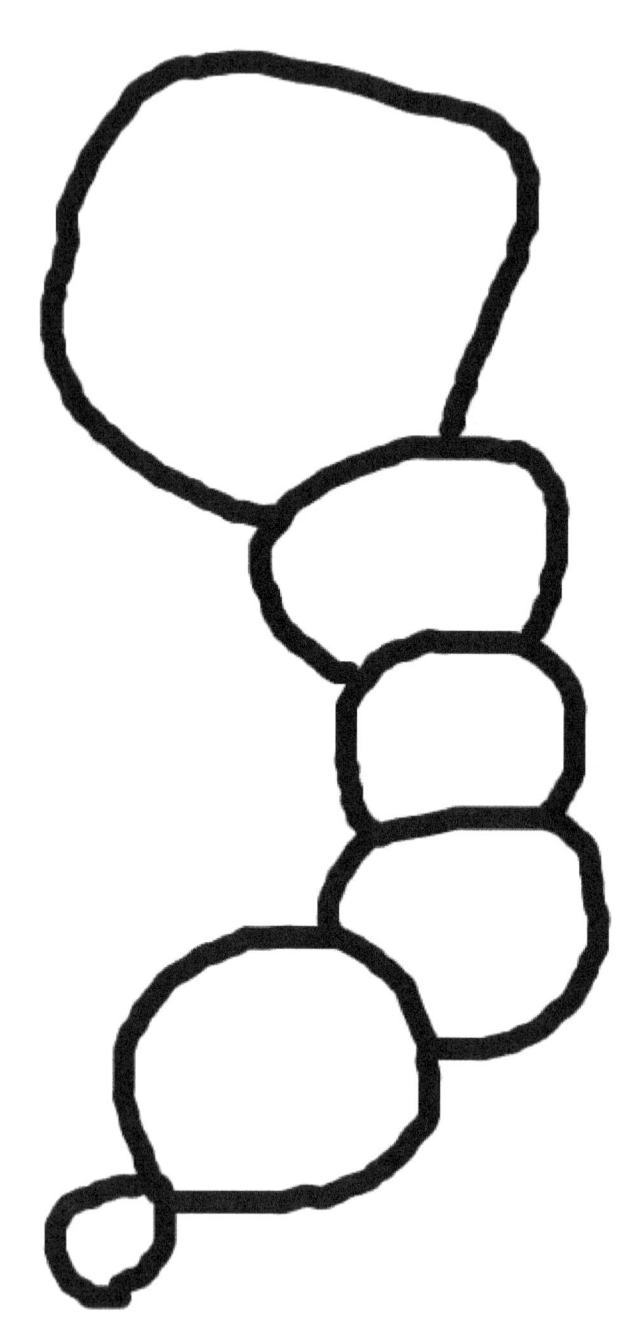

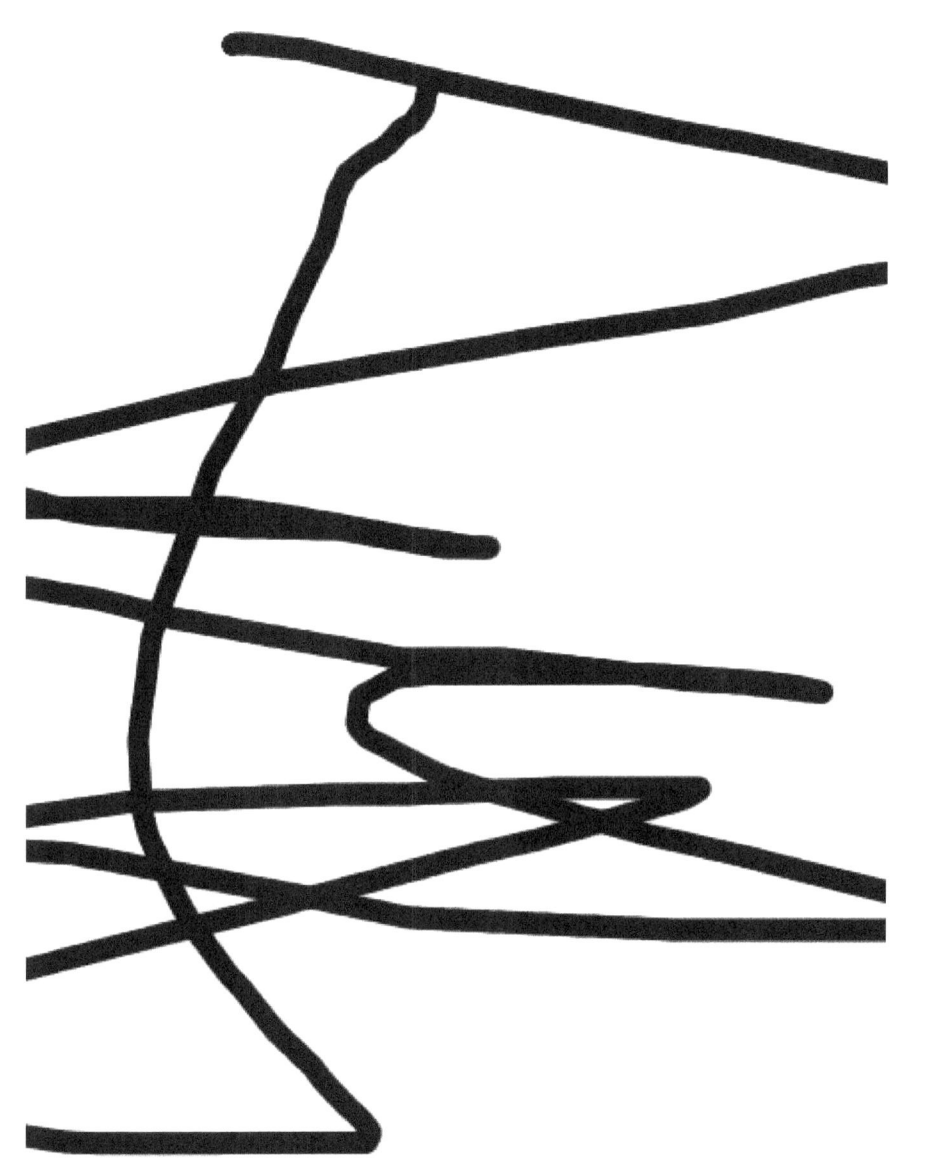

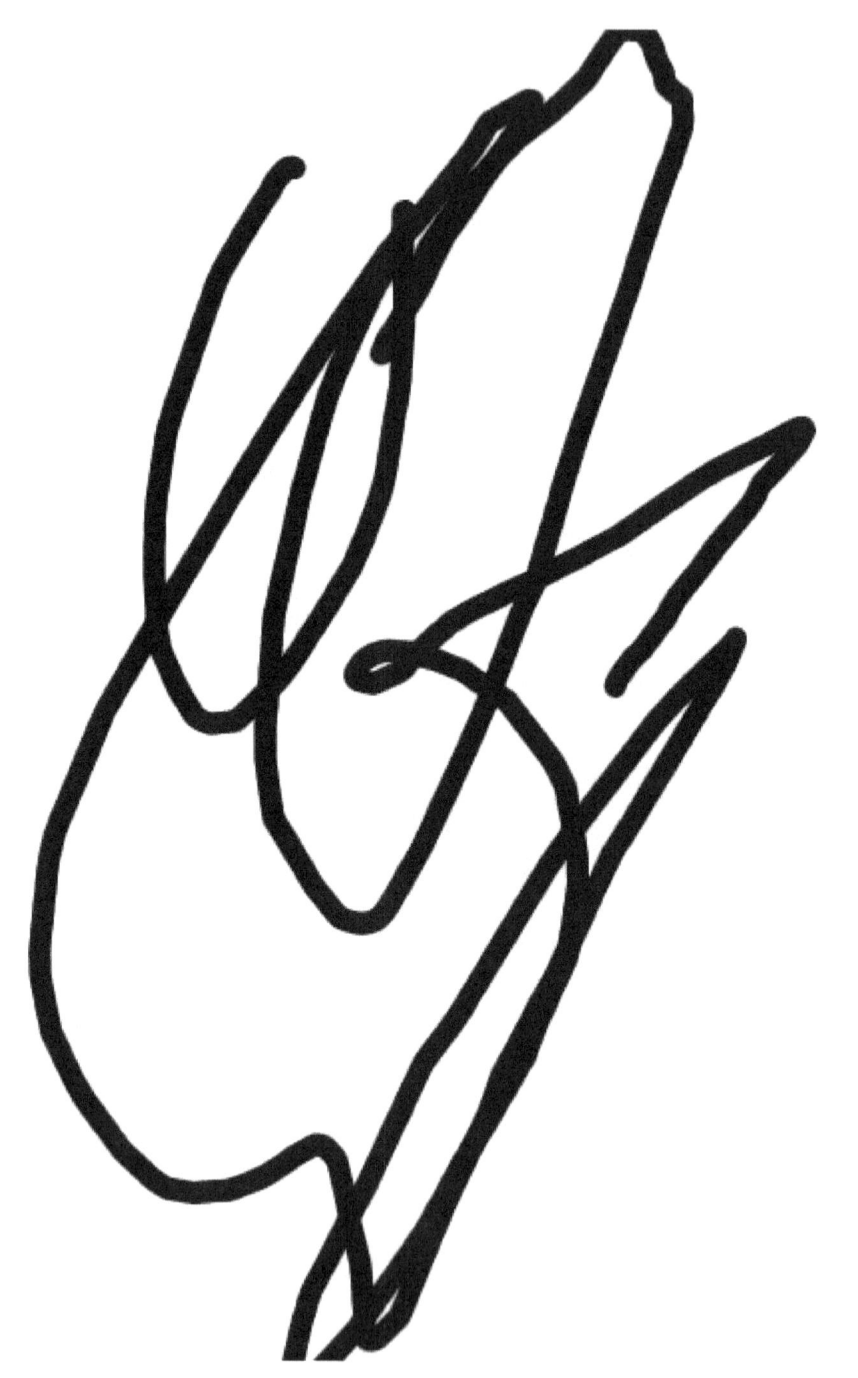

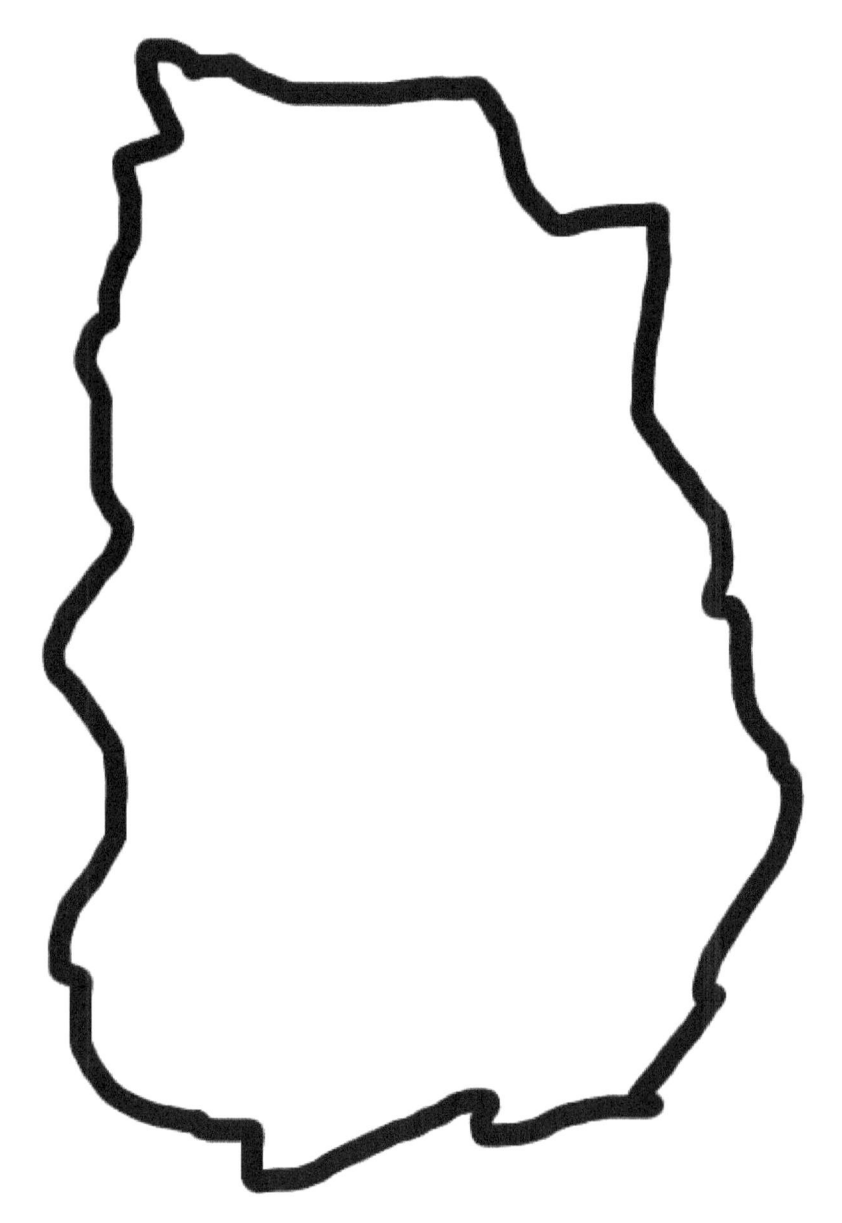

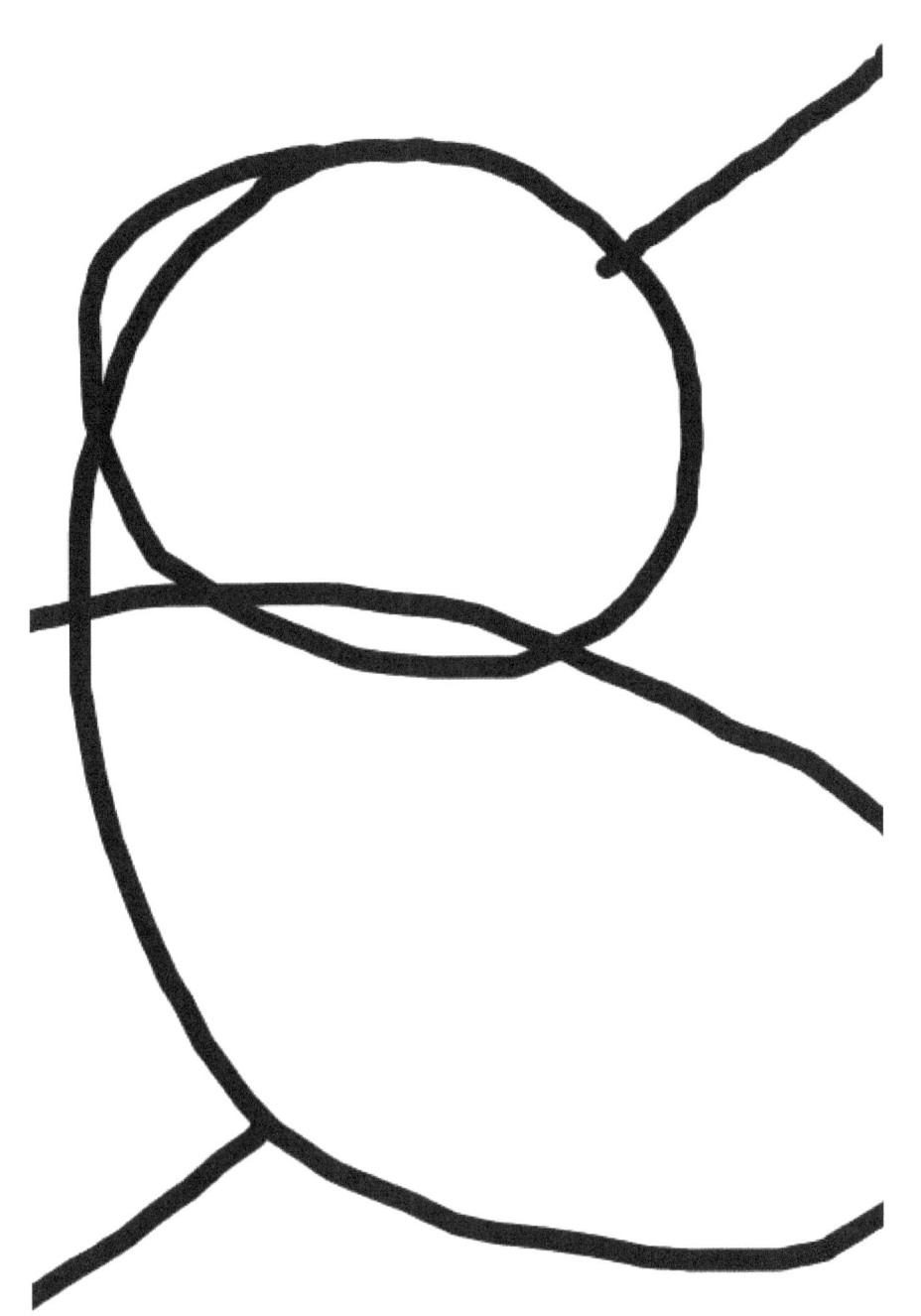

www.ingramcontent.com/pod-product-compliance
Lightning Source LLC
Chambersburg PA
CBHW071813170526
45167CB00003B/1291